Sitār and Its Music

About the author

The name of **Pandit Debu Chaudhuri** is synonymous with *sitār* and he is known for his inimitable style in the art of playing *sitār*, which is widely acknowledged and adorned by the connoisseurs of Indian music. Presently, he is the honorary secretary of Ustad Mushtaq Ali Khan Centre for Culture (UMAK). Formerly, he was dean, faculty of music and fine arts, University of Delhi, to which he was associated with for forty years. He has to his credit six books and a good number of papers published in various leading newspapers and magazines of repute.

Pandit Debu Chaudhuri has performed in many countries across the world. He has also recorded many popular albums and created eight new rāgas. He has won several awards including Padma Bhushan and Sangeet Natak Akademi Award.

He is widely known not only as an outstanding performer of international repute but also as a respected *guru*, author and composer.

Classical Musical Instruments from India, no. 1

Sitār and Its Music

Pandit Debu Chaudhuri
Padmabhushan Awardee

Assisted by
Prof. Anupam Mahajan
Dr. Prateek Chaudhuri

AVI Publishers

First published 1981
Revised and enlarged edition 2014

Cataloging in Publication Data--DK
[Courtesy: D.K. Agencies (P) Ltd. <docinfo@dkagencies.com>]

Chaudhuri, Debu.
Sitār and its music / Debu Chaudhuri, assisted by Anupam Mahajan and Prateek Chaudhuri. — Rev. and enlarged ed.
p. cm. (Classical musical instruments from India ; no. 1.)
ISBN 13: 978-81-927021-0-0 (Hb)
ISBN 13: 978-81-927021-1-7 (Pb)

1. Sitār music. 2. Rāgas. I. Mahajan, Anupam, II. Chaudhuri, Prateek. III. Title. IV. Series. Classical musical instruments from India ; no. 1.

DDC 787.82193 23

Published by:
Avi Publishers
Publishing with Rhythm
A-18, Mohan Garden
Near Nawada Metro Station
New Delhi–110 059
Phone: 011-2537-1324
e-mail: info@avipublishers.com
Web: www.avipublishers.com

Printed at: Salasar Imaging Systems, Delhi – 110 035

Dedicated to

my wife

Dr. Manjusree Chaudhuri

Brief Account of the Life and Heredity of Ustad Mushtaq Ali Khan

"Sitār Sudhakar"

Upto the 1960s India was a feudal society. The rich were very rich, the poor were mired in abject poverty. There was hardly any middle class. However, India's history of thousands of years has seen a great many economic, sociological and cultural changes of the extreme order. A few constants have always been there, affected but not much, by the changing environments of our socio-economic and political structures. One of these constants to withstand the pulls and pressures of such changes was our traditional arts — particularly music.

The credit for this dynamic insulation from all such upheavals and the constant evolution of the arts goes to the succession of extraordinary artistes India has produced over the centuries. They include such greats as Bharat Muni (second century CE), Mataṅga, Śārṅgadeva, Miāṅ Tānsen, Baiju Bawra, Adarang-Sadarang, Faiyaz Khan, Barkat-Ullah Khan,

Inayat Khan, Ashiq Ali Khan and others. They have been the backbone of the constant evolution of our classical music.

One of the recent and most illustrious names in this historical tradition is *saṅgītācārya* Ustad Mushtaq Ali Khan — a contemporary of Ustad Sadiq Ali Khan, Ustad Rahimuddin Khan, Ustad Bade Ghulam Ali Khan, Ustad Amir Khan, Prof. D.T. Joshi, and many others, but none of them are unfortunately amongst us today.

The main attribute of all these great devotees of various art forms was their unalloyed dedication to their discipline, to the exclusion of everything else. It was because of their absolute devotion that our performing arts survived, evolved and prospered even during the darkest periods of our long history.

The *guru-śiṣya paramparā* has been the mainstay of this continuity. It ensures loyalty, intensity of training and continuity of great tradition. Ustad Mushtaq Ali Khan's professional lineage descends directly in an unbroken line from Maseet Sen, the originator of Maseet Khani Baaj. Innovation, within the strict guidelines of the *rāga* system, has been the hallmark of this *gharānā*.

Born on 20 June 1911 at Varanasi, son of Ustad Ashiq Ali Khan (the disciple of Barkat-Ullah Khan — "*Aftab-e-Sitar*"), Ustad Mushtaq Ali Khan had his initial training in *sitār* from his illustrious father from the age of six.

He joined as a court musician in the then Jaunpur state in U.P. but quit early to continue his mission in life. His first major breakthrough came with the performance at the Allahabad Music Conference in 1934. After that invitations to perform multiplied and in a short time he became famous throughout the country.

Ustadji's wide repertoire of professional activities included interviews, lecture demonstrations, seminars, performances, examination and evaluations for various organizations and institutions like the All India radio (AIR), Doordarshan. His multiple activities also encompassed newspapers, books and periodicals, universities, academies, archives and societies. He also organized conferences where old masters and new artistes were introduced to the music savants as well as the general public. Among the now well-known names, Pandit Ravi Shankar of world fame was first presented by him to the public in Calcutta.

The list of his professional performances and achievements is endless. Besides the spell-binding music he performed at thousands of locations all over India, he was also a creative genius. He composed many a memorable *razakhānī gats*. He said all such compositions were natural and came from musical logic.

He always used to explain and elaborate that his principles of Seniā Gharānā was to believe in the logic of any musical application related to *rāga*. One of the principle ideas he drilled into his students was *yukti* (logic). Musical compositions flow from the logic of basic musical principles grounded in the fundamentals of the *rāga* system. Ask any of his pupils and they will emphasize the importance of logical presentation as the basis of the Seniā Gharānā. That is why he always used to say, "Seniās were *yukti vādī*". This signifies that if any Seniā performer is applying a note in a peculiar way that should be maintained as the way of application by the Seniās. For example, the application of komal *re* in Rāga Deśakār is only performed by Seniā. No wonder, he was called the musician's musician. He had his own inimitable way of interpreting our theory of music. He used to emphasize the famous statement of *uttama gānā, madhyama bājanā* as *uttama gānā, mādhyama* (as medium) *bājanā*.

Some of his most prominent students include the author Nirmal Guha Thakurta and Netai Bose (the seniormost disciple, passed away recently), Sadhan Ghosh, Prateek Chaudhuri,

Sharmistha Ghosh, Indrani Chakravorty, Anupam Mahajan and Ravi Sharma, etc.

However, as the bulk of the expansion in music simply pandered to the masses, not much effort was being made to bring our rich and sophisticated musical heritage to our people. This greatly saddened the Ustadji. Since it was impossible for him to dilute the absolute purity of traditional Indian classical music and especially of his own *gharānā*, he took up the mission of its own propagation and introduced the now rapidly expanding circle of cognoscenti, who he hoped would enable it to percolate and reach others.

In a long professional career spanning over sixty years, many professional awards and distinctions were conferred on him. He however, being a traditionalist, who refused to submit to bureaucratic whims and fancies, political awards were denied to him. Among the numerous professional distinctions conferred on him were:

Sitar Sudhakar (1932), National Academy Award (1968), Tantri Vailas (1973), Sangeet Ratnakar (1974), Hony. D. Litt (1974) State Academy Award (1974, 1989), Senior Fellowship and Emeritus (1986), Bhuwalka Award (1987), Tansen Award (1987), Special Honour (1987, University of Delhi).

Even in the evening of his illustrious career, he and his loving wife Begum Kaniz Khatoon were actively involved in a variety of projects. His departure for his heavenly abode on 21 July 1989 left a huge void in the realms of our traditional music. He has left behind many worthy student disciples who are now engaged in establishing a center in Jasola, Delhi, in the name of their *guru* as a tribute to him and to keep his music and memory alive.

On 23 December 2004 our revered Guru Mā also left us leaving behind only Khan Sahib's nephews, who are now settled in Kolkata.

Vasant Panchami **Pandit Debu Chaudhuri**
15 Feburary 2013

Foreword
(Revised Edition)

We have gone through the book written by Pandit Debu Chaudhuri titled *Sitār and Its Music*. It is no wonder that his book published thirty years ago on the same subject was appreciated widely and was in great demand. It also was a reference book on instrumental music in many universities in India where music is taught. We understand there is a persistent demand of this book and he has spent time to bring out a revised publication adding some new information for the benefit of the students.

We have known Pandit Debu Chaudhuri since he was a teacher at University of Delhi in the faculty of music and fine arts, in the early 1960s (since its inception). Though he has now retired after forty years of teaching which gave him enough experience about the numerous problems of the students of music. There are very few authors on music who also happen to be performers of high standard, and that is why this book is written keeping in mind the issues related to learning of *sitār* in any institution.

Pandit Debu Chaudhuri is a devoted student of Ustad Mushtaq Ali Khan Sahib of Seniā Gharānā. He has now wholeheartedly taken up the mission of conveying the instrumental aspect of Indian music in relation to *sitār* playing which will certainly benefit largely the students of music and that of *sitār* in particular. Many people may not know that Debu Chaudhuri, while working in University of Delhi, had also been engaged in teaching of theory also. Although he is widely known as a performer he also has an outstanding record of guiding around forty Ph.D scholars. It is no mean achievement to have guided as many students of music for the degree of philosophy in music as well as performing and writing books on music with equal zeal.

One quite interesting chapter to read is where he has dealt with the subject of *gharānā*. Here he has tried to touch upon, in brief, the *gharānā*'s contribution to the existing and traditional scenario of Indian classical music which could be a subject of interest to the students of music today and in the days to come. In some other chapters, he has brilliantly covered certain aspects of our music including *rāga*s, *tāl*s, and *gharānā*s, especially the Seniā Gharānā. Indian musicology cannot be complete without the mention of Seniā Gharānā, and we fortunately happen to know his *guru* Ustad Mushtaq Ali Khan Sahib, a true representative of Seniā Baaj, who passed away in the year 1989. Khan Sahib was a staunch follower of the Seniā style and never scarificed his style for the convenience or for the sake of public appreciation. That is why we find that the author has all the while tried to maintain the principles followed by his revered *gurujī*.

We have no hesitation in saying that this book will be of a great help for many in India and abroad not only because of the practical aspects but also the theoretical aspects as well. While talking of theory the author is particularly aware of the fact that it is not a book on theory but is meant for those who are not initiated to the art of *sitār* playing or are yet to be initiated in the art of classical music. While reviewing the book we were simply charmed that he has not attempted a controversial work but has tried to focus on the subject from the academic point of view. The author has given a very interesting account about the *sitār* and its technique and other nuances. We both are happy to note that he has made the text easy to read and understand and explained things in a very simple manner.

We feel great pleasure in writing the foreword for this book which will be a great asset for the students of Indian music and all those who intend to learn and know about *sitār* and classical music.

New Delhi
07 May 2010

Ustad Fahimuddin Khan Dagar
(Famous Druvpad Exponent)

Ustad Asad Ali Khan
(Famous Beenkar)

Foreword
(First Edition)

Sitār and Its Music by Debu Chaudhuri is a projection of his long and devoted pursuit of music. Indeed, Debu has, now, after more than thirty-five years of living with music, reached a point of advantage where the sitār with its techniques and potentials and *rāga*s with their subtleties and ethos have all become part and parcel of his very being.

Debu has learnt well, he has performed widely and with eminence; and has taught with credit. While he has all respect and regard for tradition and has great devotion for his *guru*, he also has an enquiring and analyzing mind.

It is against this background that his book *Sitār and Its Music* acquires a unique significance and becomes a truly welcome event in the context of teaching and learning of Hindustani Music with sitār as the medium, both in India and abroad.

Running into four sections, the book starts with a brief account of "Indian Musical Instruments" through the ages. Moving on to a detailed description of the structure of the sitār, chapter 2 goes on to explain and spell out the different facets of *sitār* techniques right from the stance or position in the holding and handling of the instrument to the actual production and movement of sound with its varied manifestations. This chapter is enlivened with profuse and vivid photo illustrations demonstrating the major and minor details of primary importance. These illustrations, together with their verbal descriptions, can be of immense help in understanding the actual do-how of the practice. Were these to be accompanied by their counterpart in recorded sound, the overall value and utility would be further enhanced. Debu might consider addition of such a completely documented complex for his future publications.

The remaining three chapters deal with basic elements of Hindustani Music, an outline of ten basic *rāga*s with compositions, followed by a fascinating account of a few newly-devised *rāga*s and new angles and avenues in some of the already established *rāga*s.

It is great pleasure and a proud privilege for me to commend and forward to the world of music *Sitār and Its Music* by "Debu", my esteemed friend and colleague.

29 August 1981

Sumati Mutatkar
Dean, Faculty of Music & Fine Arts
University of Delhi, Delhi

Preface

I feel great privilege in presenting this work to the readers of Indian music. There have been lot many books on Indian music written earlier, but very few are written on *sitār* and its profound facets.

It was a great dilemma for me when I started writing my first book on *Sitār and Its Technique* some forty years ago; I was not sure as to how the readers would accept my attempt, especially the students of music. After the release of the book in the year 1981, it was an immediate success and the first edition was out of print within few months. Eversince I have been receiving requests from India and abroad for copies to be mailed, but unfortunately because of my preoccupation, I could not attend to the issue. As dean and head of the department of music, University of Delhi, I had the added responsibilities to look after the department as an administrator and a *guru* as well. In addition I also had to carry on my profession as a torch-bearer of the Seniā Gharānā by propagating and performing in India and abroad.

The new work, in a way, is a revised edition of the book *Sitār and Its Technique* published earlier. I have also added some new chapters and more information based on my later research work. During this period I have been receiving many queries on my book, I realized that I must bring out a fresh updated edition particularly so as this book has been prescribed as a reference book in many universities in India and abroad. I often recieve demand letters from these institutions for the book.

My attempt has been to make this book more attractive and easy to understand for the students of music, both Indian and foreign. Whatever I have written in this book, has come from my experience as a student learning from my esteemed *gurujī* Ustad Mushtaq Ali Khan and as a teacher in the faculty of music, University of Delhi. While rewriting this book, I have altered some earlier chapters and added some new information wherever required, keeping in my mind its absolute usefulness for the students who want to learn *sitār* and our great tradition. In the last chapter I have also included eight new *rāga*s composed by me. Some of them have been widely appreciated by the connoisseurs of art and many musicians, including my students, have been performing and practising them.

Whatsoever I have tried to convey in this edition, I always kept various aspects of the *gharānā* and the teachings of my *gurujī* uppermost in my mind. I would feel extremely satisfied if my purpose of this work helps the students, musicians and other readers who are keen to know the various aspects of playing *sitār*.

This book is an attempt to convey the basic principles and other related information on *sitār* and its music. I have not tried to make everyone a master nor have I tried to convey everything through this work. One may find some relevant topics or some other information missing but I confess that it is not deliberate and sincerely feel that many more things on the subject can be incorporated in the future edition.

I hope I will, after having the requisite feedback from my readers and critics, try to do much better in the days to come.

I would be failing in my duties if I do not pay due regards to my revered *gurujī* the late Ustad Mushtaq Ali Khan Sahib who has been a great source of inspiration in my life. Though he taught me music, he also taught me how to respect and maintain the sanctity of our age-old Seniā tradition, playing *sitār* with 17 frets only. I have also been taught to respect other *gharānā*s and that is why I have refrained from making any comments on topics which could result in unnecessary controversies.

Finally, I would like to express my gratitude to my son Prateek Chaudhuri and my daughter-in-law Runa Chaudhuri who inspired me to bring out this new edition. I would also like to express my gratitude to my students Ravi Sharma, and Panchali Nandi for editing the manuscript and helping me to bring out this edition which perhaps would have not been possible without their sincere devotion and effort.

I am also indeed grateful to Shalaj Mittal, and the editors at the Avi Publishers for taking great pains and also accepting my delays in completing the edited version.

As an author I have tried my best and shall keep on trying so because it is about the music, which I call the "ocean of music" that cannot be fathom just in one life!

Debu Chaudhuri
(Padmabhushan Awardee)
Former Dean and Head
Faculty of Music and Fine Arts
University of Delhi

Key to Transliteration

VOWELS

अ a (Roman)	आ ā (palm)	इ i (it)	ई ī (police)	उ u (put)	ऊ ū (rule)	ऋ ṛ (rig)	ॠ ṝ[1]
ऌ ḷ (able)	ॡ ḹ[1]	ए e (there)	ऐ ai (aisle)	ओ o (no)	औ au (loud)		

CONSONANTS

Guttural	क ka (skate)	ख kha[2] (blockhead)	ग ga (gate)	घ gha[2] (ghost)	ङ ṅa (sing)
Palatal	च ca (chunk)	छ cha[2] (catch him)	ज ja (john)	झ jha[2] (hedgehog)	ञ ña (bunch)
Cerebral	ट ṭa (start)	ठ ṭha[2] (anthill)	ड ḍa (dart)	ढ ḍha[2] (godhead)	ण ṇa (under)
Dental	त ta (path)	थ tha[2] (thunder)	द da (that)	ध dha[2] (this)	न na (numb)
Labial	प pa (spin)	फ pha[2] (philosophy)	ब ba (bin)	भ bha[2] (abhor)	म ma (much)
Semi-vowels	य ya (young)	र ra (drama)	ल la[3] (luck)	व va[4] (vile)	
Sibilants	श śa[5] (shove)	ष ṣa[5] (bushel)	स sa (so)	ह ha (hum)	
Others	क्ष kṣa (kṣatriya)	त्र tra (triśūla)	ज्ञ jña (jñānī)		

अं (ं) ṁ anusvāra is a nasal off-glide that immediately follows the pronunciation of a vowel as in saṁskṛti.

अः visarga = ḥ consists in abrupt release of breath after a vowel as in prātaḥ.

ऽ avagraha shows non-pronunciation, that is, deletion of "a" after "e" or "o" as in ime, vasthitāḥ. In Vedic Sanskrit, it can also show word division.

HINDI LETTERS (extras)

ँ = m̐ (candrabindu)	ं = ṅ (anusvāra)	ड़ = ṛa	ढ़ = ṛha

1 Longer form of the preceding vowel.

2 Aspirated forms of the preceding consonants. The compound words given as examples should be pronounced without a syllabic break at the underlined places. "tha" and "pha" should not be pronounced as fricatives.

3 retroflexed and written "L" as "la" in certain phonetic contexts.

4 Pronounced like "w", without aspiration.

5 "śa" is palatal; "ṣa" cerebral or retroflex.

Contents

1

Indian Musical Instruments from Vedic Age to Present Day

A Brief Survey

Musical instruments have played a predominant role in the evolution and development of Indian music. In order to study the musical instruments of the present day, tracking their history becomes essential.

Indian culture and society is governed by religion and philosophy. We see the impact of religion on every aspect of Indian culture. Probably, for this very reason in Hindu mythology the invention of musical instruments was attributed to gods and goddesses. Since myth — over a period of time — has been replaced by history, therefore, it is no longer believed that gods and goddesses are the creators of these instruments. Modern scholars are of the opinion that instruments were developed and evolved with the gradual changes of civilizations.

In comparison to other countries of the world, the history of musical instruments is more exposed in the texts and sculptures of India. Music and musical instruments in their primitive forms are still in vogue with the tribals and the classical styles are thriving among the professional musicians. During the course of the last hundred years, some particular dynasties not only made the classical music popular but also made the masses aware of our rich cultural heritage. From the very beginning, vocal music and the musical instruments have been playing an important role in Indian cultural life.

These musical forms were inevitable in religious rites, court ceremonies and private entertainments. Thus, the Hindus made their gods so fond of music that it compelled Lord Śiva to say that not the thousand baths in the holy Ganges, nor the prayers may impress Him. He only loves those who sing and play for Him.

The musical instruments of the present day are the outcome of the dedication of various civilizations. From time to time, different cultural groups have influenced the development of various kinds of instruments. Not only this but the influence and impact of other countries have played a significant role in the gradual modification of these instruments. In an environment of give and take some instruments from India have travelled outside whereas some have migrated from other countries to India. There are now a number of instruments which have become a major part of the family of Indian instruments. Within India too, certain instruments are associated with different communities or human races. The polished and sophisticated look of the instruments which we find today have undergone various changes at different points of time.

We hardly find any evidence of the presence of musical instruments in the primitive age, except for the bow, which is still available with some of the tribes of India. We have, however, found some authentic pictures of musical instruments like *ḍhol, dundubhi, jhāñj*, different bow-shaped harps, long and huge drums, etc. of the Indus Valley Civilization in Moheṅjo-Dāṛo and Haṛappā.

We get a clear picture of musical instruments of the Vedic Age from the old texts available. In the *R̥gveda*, different types of string instruments and drums are mentioned along with the flutes. The other Vedas also support the *R̥gveda*. The instruments like *bana* or *śatatantrī vīṇā* (100-stringed chordophone), *nadi, veṇu, karkari, godhā, aghāti, dundubhi, bhūmi dundubhi, picchola,* etc. were used at the time of religious ceremonies. Whenever the priests used to perform the religious rites or *yajñas* they would offer *soma-rasa* to gods along with the music and chanting of the Vedic *mantras*. The Śikṣās, Prātiśākhyas and Brāhmaṇas used to guide people regarding the rules and regulations governing the composition and recital of songs. The wives of the priests were supposed to accompany them with some of the instruments mentioned above, including the *bān* which was considered the superiormost among all the *vīṇās*. The structural form of *bān* was described like that of a human body.

The notes of the Vedic songs are used in different names and manners in comparison to Laukika or Gandharva music. *Nāradīya Śikṣa* describes the differences between the names of the Vedic notes and Gandharva (music other than Vedic or Śamik) notes. This shows that the notes mentioned about *vīṇā* or flute, and the Vedic notes are mentioned as *prathama, dvitīya, tṛtīya, caturtha, mandra, atisvara* and *kruṣṭa*. Gandharva notes include *madhyama, gandhāra, ṛṣabha* (*ṛṣav*), *ṣaḍja* (*ṣaḍaj*), *dhaivata, niṣada* (*niṣad*) and *pañcama*, respectively.

In *Nāṭyaśāstra,* Bharata (third-century CE) describes music in chapters 28-34. He starts the 28th chapter with the description of musical instruments and stresses their importance, mainly the chordophones. He assembles voice under "Tatakutapa" (orchestra concerning with the string instruments). Bharata describes a few chordophones, like *vīṇā* or *mattakokila, citra, vipañci, kacchapī* and *ghoṣā*; a few aerophones like flutes, *śaṅkhī, tundakinī*, etc. A few membranophones like *mṛdaṅga, paṇava, dardura, tripuṣkaras*, etc. and idiophones like *mañjīrā, cimaṭā* and *khartāl*, etc.

Dattila and Mataṅga delineate Bharata in their books *Dattilam* and *Bṛhaddeśī,* respectively. It is believed that during Mataṅga's time, another way of singing other than Mārga style was developed and appreciated by people. It was called *Deśī*. Mataṅga's main aim was to elaborate Deśī style and he thus described *deśī rāgas, deśī tāls, deśī vādyas, deśī prabandhas*, etc. after a brief study of Mārga of Gandharva style. That is why, the name of his book is *Bṛhaddeśī* (i.e. knowledge of Deśī or popular style).

Śāraṅgadeva (thirteenth century CE) gives a broad and real picture of music studied by his predecessors. Through *Saṅgīta-Ratnākara* we come to know about the *deśī rāgas, tāls, vādyas* which are missing in *Bṛhaddeśī* today. It is believed that the first instrument with frets was invented by Mataṅga called "Kinnarī". The "Kinnarī" was used both in Mārga and Deśī styles of music. Śāraṅgadeva describes a few more fretted instruments, viz. *ālāpinī, tritantrī jantra,* etc. He also defined some more chordophones, such as, *pinākī and sāraṅgī*. The most important *vīṇā,* he describes is *ekatantrī* or *ghoṣā*. According to him, after seeing or touching it, people can enjoy heavenly bliss.

Besides the chordophones, Śāraṅgadeva mentions a few types of flutes, *mṛdaṅga, mardala, paṇava, kahala, dardura, tāl, kartāl,* etc. in detail. Later, Rāṇā Kumbhā (fifteenth century CE) also describes the above instruments including some other new instruments of his time.

During the tenth-eleventh centuries, Muslim invaders invaded India and expanded their regime. They defeated most of the free states. Thus, the whole of India was disturbed frequently and its social, political and cultural set-up was thoroughly shaken. Only a few emperors, from time to time, tried to take interest to revive the rich socio-cultural fabric again. As far as music is concerned, we get only a few evidences of the emperors, who took interest in it. We can name only two dynasties in this regard; these are Khalji and Mughal dynasties. Alauddin Khalji was very fond of music and the great maestros like Gopal Nayak and Amir Khusro were in his court. In the Mughal dynasty, mainly during the period of Akbar the Great and some later emperors, music flourished. Tānsen, who is known as father of north Indian music, was one of the *navratnas* (gems) of the Akbar's court.

The *bīn, jantar, rabāb, mukhbīn, chāṅg, pakhāwaj, ḍholak, śehnāī, vaṁśī, kartāl, mañjirā,* etc. are described in *Āin-i-Akbarī*. But the book does not make any mention of most of the ancient instruments.

One may note that the traditions of music and musicians are linked mainly with Miāṅ Tānsen, the great maestro of music after Gopal Nayak. Most of the musicians, whether they are vocalists or *bīn, rabāb, sarod,* or *sitār* players link themselves with Seniā Gharānā, named after Tānsen and his successors. The tradition is believed to have percolated either directly from Tānsen and his sons or from his daughter's family or from the teacher-taught linkage (*guru-śiṣya paramparā*).

During the last days of the Mughal empire, the *sitār* was developed. This instrument, according to some scholars, was known previously as *jantar* which was the popular name of *tritantrī*, an ancient instrument.

During the eighteenth to twentieth centuries, this instrument slowly became popular and students of music started learning and practising it all the more Moreover, yet another style of singing evolved which was named Khyāl and was introduced as an alternative to Dhrupad. *Sitār* took the place of *vīṇā*. *Vīṇā* was also used to accompany Dhrupad.

But incidentally *sitār* was not developed as an accompaniment of voice. Like Khyāl singing and its tradition (*gharānā*), sitārists also made their own style of playing which was called *bāj*. Thus, the style of playing the *sitār* did not entirely depend on vocal compositions but it developed its own way of playing. There are two kinds of *bāj*, or styles, called *masit khanī* and *razā khanī*. *Masit khanī* composition (*gat*) was introduced by Ustad Masit Sen of Delhi. He was the descendant of Tānsen. The tempo here is slow and strokes (*bols*) are fixed. The starting point is also fixed. The *razā khanī* composition (*gat*) was introduced by Ustad Razā

Khan of Lucknow. The tempo here is fast, and there is no hard and fast rule of starting from a particular beat. But the starting points of old compositions were, generally, either from 9th, 7th, 1st or 12th beat. Nowadays, some more starting points of a *bandiś* have developed, such as 14th, 15th, 5th, 8th, etc. in a cycle of sixteen beats (*tīntāl*), by some of the creative artists.

Some more instruments other than *sitār* were also developed side by side, viz. *surbahār, rabāb, sarod, sāraṅgī, surśṛṅgār, śehnāī,* etc.

Today, we come across with some more modern instruments other than the above-mentioned ones such as *vichitra vīṇā (batta bīn), santūr,* violin, *jaltaraṅg, naltaraṅg, kaṣṭhataraṅg, kāñchtaraṅg, tablatāraṅg, flute, tār śehnāī, ḍholak, pakhāwaj, ḍhol, tablā, mañjirā, kartāl* and so on. It seems that some of the instruments were derived from the other, whereas some were newly invented; some even changed their original names and shapes. Some of the instruments have migrated from other countries that gave a new dimension to its richness. Very few artistes choose to take up those instruments which are not popular, as a result some of these have now become obsolete. Instruments like *sitār, sarod* and *tablā* today dominate the performing field of music. This does not construe that the instruments which are not in vogue are not good. In the modern times, some Indian musicians and the students are looking at music as a commercial proposition which is a matter of deep regret. As a result, the instruments, which are popular, are becoming more popular and instruments which are not popular are being pushed to the oblivion. A time may come when these instruments will only remain as museum showpieces, as a result of the partisan attitude of the performers, students and listeners. The popularity of instruments unfortunately depends on the listeners and today it entirely depends on the desire and liking of the general masses, although it is a subject of discussion whether this has done good to our music or not.

2

The Sitār

Its Features and Playing Techniques

Today *sitār* is not only popular in India but has acquired a place of its own in the international domain of music.

It has been made to believe by some scholars of the early twentieth century that Amir Khusro, the celebrated musician of Alauddin Khalji, the Emperor of Delhi (thirteenth century CE), is the inventor of *sitār*. This view is so much accepted and popularized by the modern writers that even the musicians of this century have not only accepted it but also propagated the same theory. However, some of the applied musicologists have made considerable research on the controversial subject and come to a conclusion that it was neither Amir Khusro, nor any other particular musician who invented this instrument, but it is instead a gradual process of development from the *tritantrī vīṇā* to *jantar*, and from *jantar*, it has taken its shape to *sitār as it is* in the present scenario. It would be interesting to note that Amir Khusro himself never claimed to be the inventor of *sitār* and *tablā* in any of his books. What is more, none of his contemporary writers have given any indication in their books written during his time.

Sitār, at present, is the most popular instrument in the Indian music. Whosoever is interested in music is quite well acquainted with the name and form of this instrument. The structure and the quality of the sound of the *sitār* of today is the result of many years of dedicated research which has improved both, its form and sound beyond recognition of what it originally was. It must be noted that both *sitār* and *sarod* of the present day have improved immensely in shape and sound due to the tremendous efforts of the manufacturers of West Bengal (Kolkata).

General Features and Structure of Sitār

The standard length of the *sitār* is approximately four feet. The finger board or the *daṇḍ* is made of a special kind of wood which is not heavy and is locally called *śīśam* wood. This is about 3 feet in length. The standard width of the *daṇḍ* is about $3^{1}/_{4}$ to $3^{1}/_{2}$ inches. The lower end of the instrument, which has the dome shaped resonating part, is made of dried gourd, known as *tumbā*. The gourd, when it assumes the appropriate size, is set aside to dry. Afterwards it is cut in the middle with a particular measurement which should be $13^{1}/_{2}$ inches minimum in width so that the *tablī* could fit in properly. *Tablī* means the part which is covered with a thick wooden base, where the bridge rests, and that is the main source of the good sound of a *sitār*. Generally, the size of the *tablī* should be $13^{1}/_{2}$ to 14 inches in length and $12^{1}/_{2}$ to $13^{1}/_{2}$ inches in width. The *daṇḍ* is joined with both the *tumbā* and the *tablī* by a block of wood and the joint is known as *gulu* or *gul*. The maker of the instrument gives it a certain shape in accordance with the specification, with the help of a chisel. Much of its sound quality depends on the craftsmanship of chiselling and each instrument gets its individual share of high precision accuracy and care and that makes the sound of one instrument different from the other. The *daṇḍ* has frets according to the style of the school (*gharānā*). Usually there are 19 frets which are standard for the modern *sitārs* but again this varies from 17 to 20 frets depending upon individual players. There are musicians who use even 22 frets in order to obviate unwanted movement of any fret in the *sitār*. Although the *sitār* players of the modern day are using 20 or 21 frets yet the traditional Seniā (from Tānsen's School) players from Jaipur prefer to play with 17 frets only even today. Ustad Mushtaq Ali Khan, the author's *guru*, is the only renowned performer in India who followed the same tradition. The illustrations given in this book thus show the *sitār* with 17 frets.

This tradition of frets goes back to the time of Amrit Sen, the great master musician of the Seniā tradition, who was born in the eighteenth century. Those who keep frets come under another school and their system is known as *chal thāṭ*.

The frets are not flat, but curved a little to facilitate the *mīṇḍ*, i.e. deflection of the string through the fret. These are made of thick metal wire (German steel) and are tied to the *daṇḍ* with silk thread, catgut or nylon fishing line. As the frets are easily movable, the player can choose any scale he wants.

The seven strings are fixed and tied in corresponding pegs (*khūṇṭī*) at one end and pass through the *tār gaheṅ*, an ivory plate with holes for strings to pass through and then over the *daṇḍ* and the bridge to the other end. Then it is tied with a loop at the end called *laṅgoṭ*, which is made of ivory, bone, wood or brass in the modern days. The *laṅgoṭ* is fixed with a screw with the *tumbā* and *tablī*. The pegs are inserted at the other end of the *daṇḍ* and also used for tuning the strings.

The bridge is placed on the heart of the *tablī*. It is made of either ivory, bone or horns of deer and is called *javarī*. *Javarī* is the heart of the instrument and is fixed and placed on a wooden platform called *savarī*. To ensure the correct pitch of each string and proper levelling, two pieces of ivory or bone are fixed across the *daṇḍ* near the tuning pegs at the other end. Out of seven strings, five pass through holes and over the specified places. While the piece with holes is known as *tār gaheṅ*, the other place with cuts on it for the strings, close to pegs, is known as *meru*. The remaining two strings are passed through the two small supporting stands and two very small poles made of bone called *kīl*. To cover the wooden joints, the craftsmen make beautiful designs on them. For the purpose of the base sound for the lower octave, bronze or copper wire is used, besides the steel strings which are most common.

Strings

Traditionally, only seven strings are used out of which two must be *joṛ* and made of brass or bronze tuned in the tonic, i.e. *sa* (C), and 11 to 13 sympathetic strings. We find that the sympathetic strings were added to the *sitār* in the late nineteenth century.

The first steel string which is mostly used in the instrument is called *bāj kā tār*. It is tuned in F or *ma* but the base of the tuning is second string which is tuned to C or *sa*, the tonic note of *sitār*. The tonic note is extremely important in the Indian music because this never changes. As mentioned earlier, the *joṛ* is the basis of the traditional tuning and string arrangements. The *joṛ kā tār* is made either of brass or copper. Thus with the help of the tonic or *sa*, other strings are tuned. The second and the third strings are tuned to *sā*, fourth and fifth are in *pa* and *pa* (*mandra* and *madhya*) and the last two strings are tuned to the middle and higher octave of the tonic, which is known as *chikārī*, and the last three strings are made of steel. This system of tuning is the most traditional but changes have been made in the order of tuning by the musicians of today.

The old and new systems of the tuning of *sitār* have something in common, but musicians have made a lot of experiments on it. For example, the word *joṛ* means two strings tuned to the tonic, but now many musicians are keeping only one *joṛ* string instead of two strings. On the other hand some musicians have added the *ga* (steel string) and *pa* (steel string) instead of *mandra pañcham* (lower 5th note). Some of the musicians have added the additional long *chikārī* tuned into the middle octave *sa* (C). However, there is no doubt that the continued experiments have certainly brought a new dimension to the art of tuning a *sitār*.

The Sympathetic Strings

Sitār, with sympathetic strings (*tarab*), is very popular these days. Here the strings run parallel to the main strings under the frets. The number of strings varies from 11 to 13 on different instruments, but 13 strings are the most common today. The length of the first *tarab* string is twice the length of the last *tarab* string. The small pegs (*khūṇṭīs*) are fitted into the side of the *daṇḍ*. The *sitārs* with the sympathetic strings are known as *tarabdār sitārs*. Tuning of these strings depends upon the scale or the *rāga*, and of course, on the mood of the artist also. Usually the first *tarab* string is tuned to *sa* (C) second *ni* (B) and the third one again to *sa* (C) and then the other notes will follow accruing to the desired scale. Tuning of notes from the lower octave leads to the higher one, and is always done in the ascending order. Some musicians also tune the first string of the *tarab* in *ni* (B) format.

The Technique of Playing Sitar

The position of holding the *sitār* has varied from time to time. Since the nineteenth century to the modern period there have been five different types of sitting positions which musicians have used according to their convenience or under the guidance of the *guru*.

Some female players choose to sit in some other positions, to suit their individual convenience. Few of the female players even prefer to sit in the position of a male player. Certain particular rules are to be followed to hold the *sitār* and they are essential because they help the players to hold the instrument in the right position and give them a good grip over it. These are:

1. The *tumbā* will be placed on the heel of the left foot and right forearm should be kept firmly in such a position that it can hold the *sitār* without the help of the left hand.
2. The pressure of the right forearm should not effect the right hand wrist, thumb and the fingers, while playing.
3. The left arm should be left free so that it can move freely from the lowest to the highest notes (frets).
4. While playing, the right arm beyond the wrist should not

move and special care should be taken so that the wrist also does not move while playing.

5. The instrument should be quite close to the player's body and the holding angle should be approximately 45° from the base of the right hand side.
6. While holding the *sitār* for playing, the thumb of the right hand should be firmly fixed near the last fret and the *gulu*.

Fingering Technique of both the Hands

As I have mentioned earlier, the thumb of the right hand should be kept near the lowest fret and it must be on the side of the *daṇḍ*. The position of the thumb should be relaxed but stable. The fingers and the thumb should not be stiff but rather loose; that however does not mean that the thumb may leave its position where it should be firmly kept. The thumb should not at all move from place to place. The striking point with the *mizrāb* (plectrum) should be in between the lowest fret and the bridge, but it should be much closer to the lowest fret.

With the help of the right hand forefinger, the strings are played with strokes as *da* and *ra*. These two strokes are the basis of stroke-work and from these we have many combinations like *da, dir, dara*, etc. The first basic stroke is *da* which is in the "inward" direction, closing all fingers towards the thumb while thumb remains firm in its own position as shown in the illustrations. The second basic stroke is *ra* which goes outward striking out all the fingers straight. This flexible full movement of the fingers is very important but unfortunately many of our students of *sitār* do not realize the scientific aspect of this movement. As a result, their movement of the fingers gets restricted and they cannot produce good bold strokes later on when it is too late for rectification. Combining these two strokes, as said earlier, becomes *dir* or *diri*. This is played usually together and also at a higher speed than *da* or *ra*. To be more precise, it is played in double the speed of *da* or *ra*. The various types of strokes will be discussed in chapter three with elaborations.

Proper Position of holding the Sitār

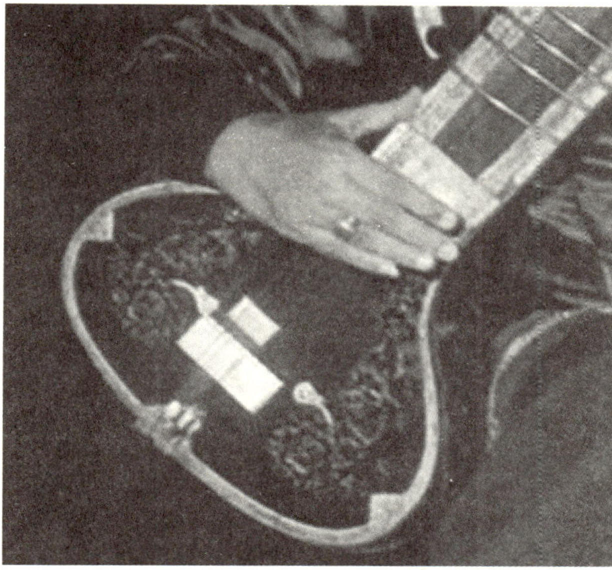

This is how to hold the *sitār*, with the right hand, keeping the thumb fixed on the *sitār* and bringing all the fingers inside to play "*da*".

The position of all the fingers after playing (striking) "*da*" should be round in shape.

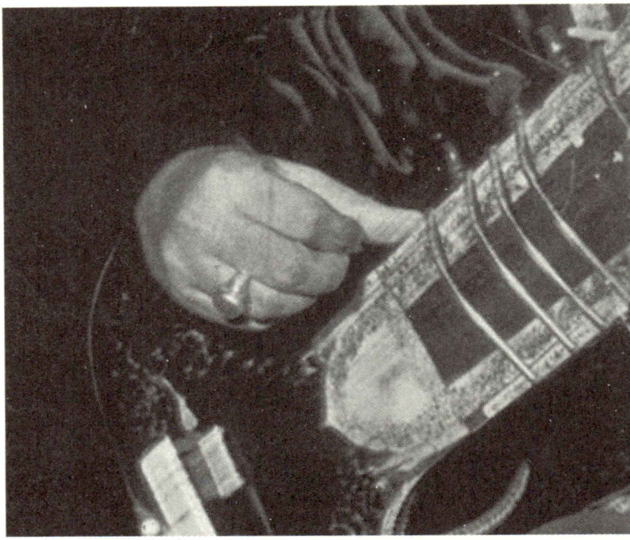

Complete movement of the fingers after striking "*da*".

Gradually folding all the fingers to play "*da*".

Wrong position of the thumb, because the thumb should remain fixed at one point.

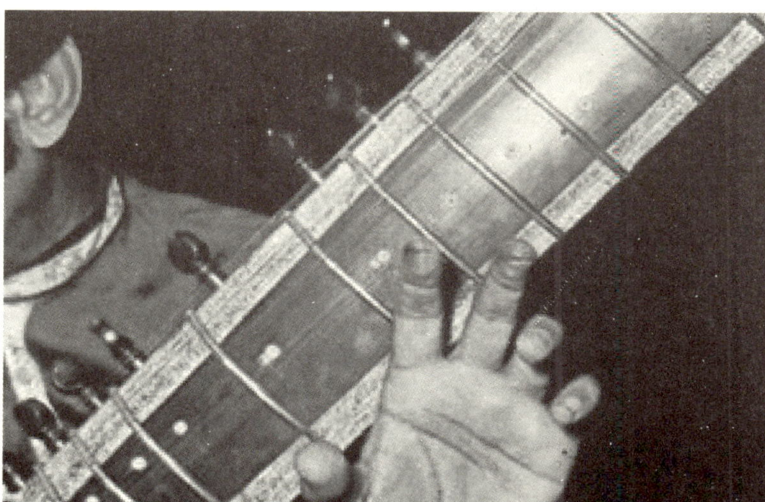

Correct placement of the left hand fingers — where the strings should be pressed.

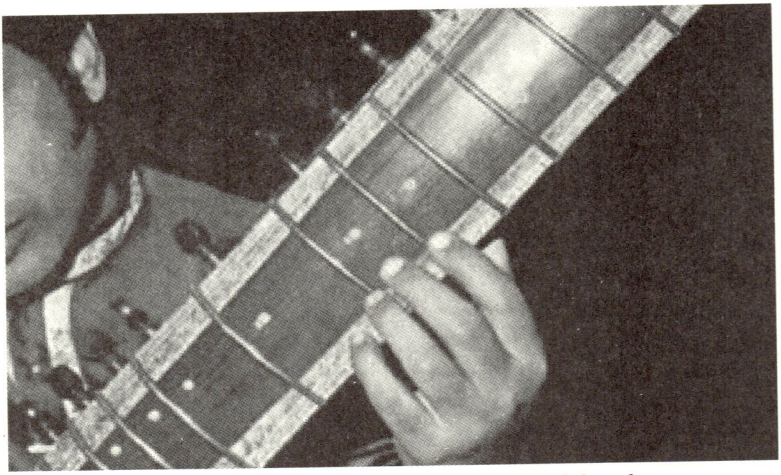

This is how to hold the *sitār* with the left hand;
it should be round shaped.

Correct positioning of the fingers of the left hand.

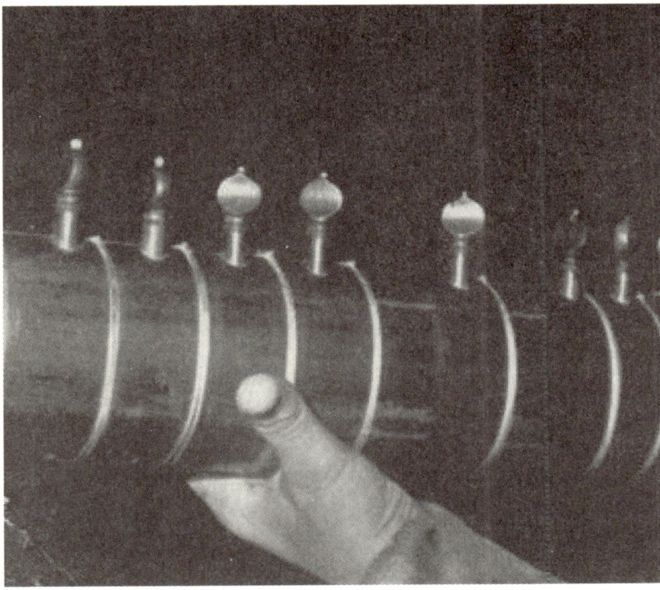

Wrong placement of the thumb

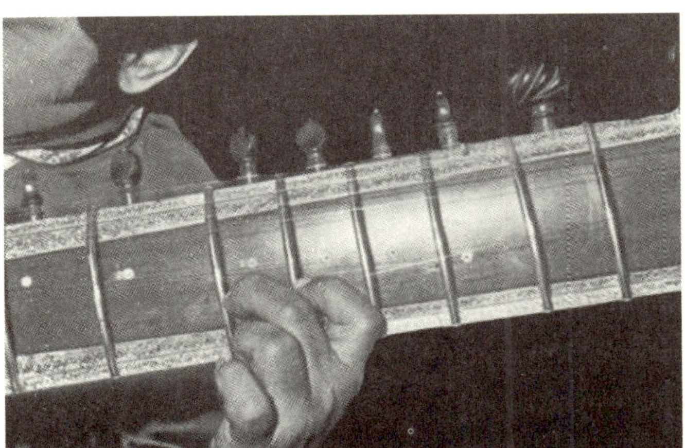

Correct position of pulling the string (*mīṇḍ*).

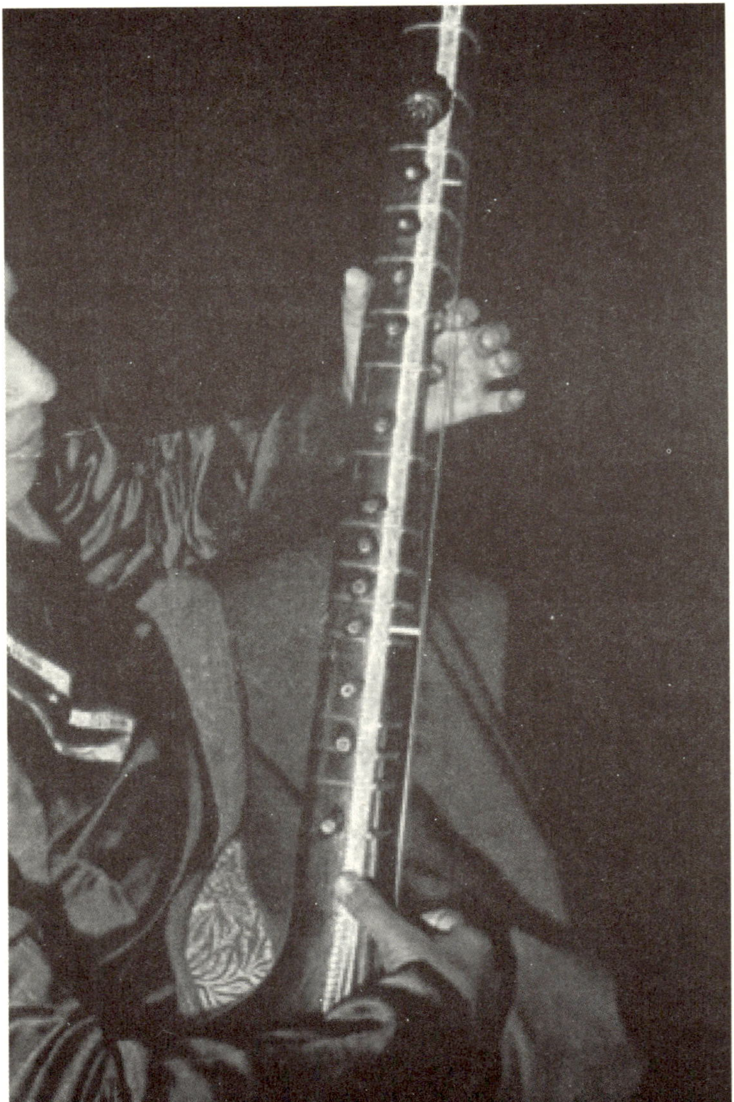

This picture shows the correct way of holding the *sitār* and placement of the thumb. Observe the thumbs of both the hands.

For the Beginners

The beginners in the field of *sitār* should remember that the fingers of both the hands should be relaxed and kept close to each other. This will help them to have a better tonal quality. The index finger of the right hand is the main finger for striking the strings but along with it the other fingers follow closely, giving them a round shape while playing *da* (the illustration shows the correct form as how to play *da*). It is very difficult to play *sitār* with only one finger (index finger); it must be avoided, otherwise there will be no flexibility in the fingers and it will be rather too difficult to play fast *tāns* (note patterns).

As for the left hand mainly two fingers are used, these are (i) the index finger and (ii) the middle finger, which are normally known by the students as the first and the second finger. Some players use three fingers too for the convenience of playing the first and the fourth note where there is a big gap, but some players prefer to stretch their first and second fingers that far with the same effect but without any strain whatsoever. The little finger of the left hand also plays an important part while playing *joṛ* or wherever a special effect of sound, *laya*, is necessary, with the first *tarab* string. The *tarab* string (the first one which is tuned in either *sa* or *ni*) gives an effect which is created by striking it with the little finger as and when it is necessary. This aspect of *sitār* playing is purely personal and much depends on the artist who plays it and he or she only can decide as where to strike and where not to.

The *tarab* strings (sympathetic strings) also help in creating an atmosphere of the tempo as well as the mood of the *rāga*.

The correct way of playing *sitār* with the first and second fingers is to be clearly understood, otherwise faulty fingering might cause a hindrance to a good performance. The tips of the fingers are to be pressed on the string just above the frets. It might be useful for the beginners to note that they have to avoid the fret slightly to produce a clear sound, otherwise if anyone places the fingertip right on top of the fret then the sound will rather be a subdued one and not a clear one. The player will have to get hold of the actual position which may be seen from the photographs for having a clear picture of the left hand fingers. The left hand thumb should be placed properly behind the neck of the instrument and it should be placed in such a way so that it does not hinder the free movement of the left hand from going up and down, that is from lower octave to the higher octave. The thumb always remains one fret above the first finger where the note is played. If the first finger is on *sa*,then the thumb should be on *ni*. The thumb should be so close to the *daṇḍ* that it can always have a good grip over the instrument.

The role of first finger is very important in playing *sitār* because it is always used both in the ascending and the descending order (*ārohī* and *avrohī*), and it is never taken off while playing the instrument. The second finger is used as a helping finger while coming back from any note, e.g. R G M P M G R S. Here the second finger will be used on *pa* (fifth note). The second finger is also used while playing *mīṇḍ*. This is done in order to help the first finger to have more strength as a support to deflect the string. This is specially done because of some players who might find it difficult to pull the string beyond three notes with one finger. In case a player wants to pull the string from *sa* to *pa* (first to fifth) from *sa* itself, it might be rather difficult because it requires a lot of strength of the first finger to do so. But I have seen my *guru* doing it, which is a rare thing indeed. Some players use the third finger too, for their own convenience, but that may not be accepted by some of the pure traditional players.

Wearing of Plectrum (Mizrāb)

The plectrum should be worn in such a way that it should not come out easily while playing *sitār*. Even if someone else wants to take it out, he should find it difficult to do so unless the player himself takes it out. It is to be fixed firmly on the first finger (see photographs) and should remain straight. Some players prefer to keep its nose slightly towards left so as to get a better sound quality. The tip of the plectrum should project from the tip of the finger. Learners with projected nails will have a problem in fixing it properly. The upper corners should be placed just below the last joint of the first finger. The correct technique of taking out the plectrum is to slide it slowly from one side and then from the other side, but one should never try to take it out straight. This method may cause considerable pain in the joint or both sides of the first finger in due course of time. It is expected that the same plectrum is used without changing its position on the finger. It may also be noted that the plectrum when worn (*mizrāb*) must have its top side on the top position and should not be changed from top to bottom side, because that will not help in having a solid grip of the plectrum. If the plectrum is changed frequently then the player will find it difficult to play properly because of more pain due to change in position. Wearing a plectrum is as important as the proper placement of left hand fingers on the frets. These two things should not be ignored at all by the beginners.

Adjustment of Frets (Pardās)

*Sitār*s, that have 17, 19 or 20 frets, need the adjustment of frets, depending on the requirements of the particular scale required for a *rāga* to be played. The frets are usually tied up on the natural scale and any change to minor scale (specially for *komal re* or *komal dha* corresponding to minor second and minor sixth note) needs to be adjusted upwards. The desired note *komal re* or *komal dha* could be found in between the frets *sa* and *re* and *pa* and *dha*. One can easily see the gap in between these two notes. The way to shift the fret to its desired place is to hold the *sitār* upwards in a standing position and move both ends of the fret with the right hand thumb and second finger and left hand thumb and second finger simultaneously and gently. The movement of the fingers should be smooth. While moving the frets, the nail of the left hand thumb may be used to move the guts slowly so that it does not break or comes out of the fret. But the movement should be upward from one side and then the other side, but never simultaneously.

Replacement of Strings

In a *tarabdār sitār*, replacing the main strings is required more frequently than replacing the sympathetic strings (*tarab ke tār*).

While replacing the main string, first of all pull out the peg (*khūṇṭī*) and remove the remaining broken part of the string from the peg. Take the string, measure its length. But preferably one should keep six to ten inches extra than the required length, then make a small loop by giving eight to ten turns to the string and fix it on the other end of the *tumbā* on the *laṅgoṭ* and take out the other clean end through the *tār gaheṅ* and *meru*. Then insert the string (pass it) through the small hole (like a thread in the needle) of the peg and place the peg in its own place. While putting the peg in its own place, see that the peg is placed on the other small hole on the *daṇḍ*. The inner end hole in the *daṇḍ* is bigger than the outer end hole of the *daṇḍ*. Then put your right hand on the loose string to avoid any twist in the string and with the left hand start turning the peg and then tune it. Remember that a new string takes some time to stay on a particular note, as desired, so it is advised that the string may be pulled on the fret a number of times before playing the *sitār*.

Replacing the *tarab* strings is more difficult and complicated, and you have to study the system very carefully before trying it out practically. First of all, pull out the peg as mentioned earlier and take out the broken piece of the string and then insert the unlooped side of the string through the hole on the finger board below the frets corresponding to the hole of the peg taken out. Take a thick wire or a hair pin and hook its one end like a fishing hook so that it can go easily through the hole of the peg. Insert the hook into the hole and try to hook out the wire which you have put in earlier through the hole on the finger board. Thread it through the small hole of the peg and give it one or two turns and put it back again to its place. Then take the other end of the string and make a loop as stated earlier and take the loop-end under the frets and under the large upper bridge and fix it at the end on the *laṅgoṭ* (near the *tumbā*). Then once again hold the string by the middle finger of the right hand and tighten the string with the left hand by turning the peg, and finally place the string, while tightening over the small bridge (below the large bridge) accordingly; and then finally tune it to the desired note.

Maintenance of the Instrument

Sitār is one of the most delicate instruments of Indian classical music and it needs special care. The most delicate part is the *tumbā* (gourd) which may break any time if there is a slight jerk or if it is hit with a hard object. It is advisable to keep it in a box or in a protected cover for the safety and cleanliness. Dust particles may ruin its sound and the strings too. It should be cleaned everyday and the strings should be changed before they rust. For cleaning the instrument, a soft brush or a soft piece of cloth is ideal. Never use too much of oil on the main string but it must be cleaned (specially the main string) after playing and should be kept thereafter in cool temperature. It should never be kept directly under the sun. More care should be taken to protect the *javarī* (the upper bridge) of the main string. To ensure a longer life of the *javarī*, I have found that keeping a piece of fine paper on the *javarī* just below the set of strings, after playing the instrument, is very useful. This practice increases the normal life of *javarī*, thus saving the trouble of having the *javarī* replaced every month or so. It is a general practice to use oil on the main string for facilitating a free movement of the hand, specially for fast passages, but using too much oil proves to be harmful because the oil ultimately reaches the bridge, thus spoiling the sound of the *sitār* as the bridge is the "heart of the sound". Special care should be taken to protect the bridge from any damage . *Javarī* gives the continuity of the sound, which is the soul of Indian music. If the instrument is not played for some days then the strings may get rusted and this may spoil the *javarī*. The string therefore should be checked from time to time and evev replaced if it has been too much used or is rusted. It has been noticed that sometimes some players use too much of oil to have the main string greasy for quicker movement, but this causes a considerable damage to the bridge as the oil from the string comes closer to the bridge resulting in a dead sound. The best way to prevent the spill over of oil to the bridge is to wipe it out and clean the string every time after playing the *sitār*.

In each *sitār*, the bridge has a specially marked place where it rests on the *tablī* (the sound board), this position should not be changed at all. Sometimes the bridge comes off due to the dry weather, the legs of the bridge not having been glued properly. But a drop of varnish will help settle the legs of the bridge. There should preferably not be any gap between the legs of the bridge and the surface of the *tablī*. Strong adhesive should be avoided because the bridge should come out easily, whenever it is necessary to have a new levelling of the bridge which is technically known as *javarī*. Even a hair-line gap in between may give a bad sound and also cause problem for *mīṇḍ* (pulling or deflection).

Drawback of the Instrument

Although it is being termed as a drawback of the instrument but it has still been accepted in general as there is hardly any remedy. If you pull the string for the purpose of playing *mīṇḍ* by the first string, then you will observe that the second string, i.e. *joṛ* string, which is tuned in *sā* or the *tonic*, goes slightly down. Thus it becomes difficult for the musician to keep the tonic in its proper place. In India there must have been more than a million *sitār*s manufactured till now but very few are free from this defect. The reputed musicians manage this defect with remarkable skill so that the listeners will not know the difference. It is so minute in terms of frequency that generally, people are not even able to distinguish it.

During the rainy season, the pegs become hard to move because of the wood, that is not properly seasoned. As a result, the sitārist may find it difficult to tune the instrument. In such a case, try to get the peg out from the hole from the other side by slightly pushing it with a hard piece of small rod, and hitting it just at the centre of the peg at the other smaller end. Thereafter hit it gently and take it out slowly; rub the points of contact with a sand paper and then use a french chalk and put it back once again in its own place. The instrument creates more problem in a humid weather, especially in the rainy season, but during winter season it produces a very good sound. Special care must be taken to keep the *sitār* properly covered and, if possible, it should be kept tuned too.

Specialities of Seniā Gharānā

"Seniā Gharānā" is known for its tradition and purity, which dates back from the time of the great doyen of Indian classical music, Miāṅ Tānsen. The unique feature of this *gharānā* is that it follows the traditional system of music and maintains the purity of *rāgas*. This *gharānā* not only maintains the purity of *rāgas*, but it also has its own way of presenting certain *rāgas* which may sound a little bit different from the presentation of other *gharānās*. It is also unique because most of its technique is taken from the *bīn-aṅg*. The author had the good fortune of learning from his *guru* who represents this tradition of "seven generations of *sitār* players" dating back from the originator of *masit khanī bāj*, the great innovator Masit Sen. This is the only *gharānā* in India which is having seventeen frets (*pardās*) and is following the oldest tradition till today.

On the basis of scanty records available, Masit Khan (originator of *masit khanī bāj*) emerges as a direct descendant in the sixth generation from Miāṅ Tānsen. A unique feature of this tradition is that it represents an uninterrupted line of *sitār* players for eight generations. The author is fortunate enough in having a *guru*, who upheld the tradition in its truest form and spirit. Ustad Mushtaq Ali Khan, in turn, represents the tradition of Seniā Gharānā, dating back from the great Ustad Masit Sen.

Family Tree of Ustad Mushtaq Ali Khan and his Tradition

Masit Sen
↓
Bahadur Sen (son)
↓
Sukh Sen (son)
↓
Rahim Sen (son)
↓
Amrit Sen (son)
↓
Barkat-ullah Khan (*śiṣya*)
↓
Ashiq Ali Khan (*śiṣya*)
↓
Mushtaq Ali Khan (son)
↓
Debu Chaudhuri (*śiṣya*)
↓
Prateek Chaudhuri (son)

3

Hindustani Music and Elementary Techniques of Sitār

This section sets out to focus the spotlight on some basic facts of the melodic aspects of Hindustani Music as well as about the elementary techniques of *sitār* along with lessons for practice.

Hindi Script for Seven Notes

स	रे	ग	म	प	ध	नि
S	R	G	M	P	D	N
Sa	Re	Ga	Ma	Pa	Dha	Ni

Self-exercise for Identifying the Script

1.	प	म	स	नि	रे	ग	ध
2.	रे	प	म	ग	स	ध	नि
3.	ध	रे	स	नि	प	ग	म
4.	नि	स	प	रे	ध	ग	म
5.	स	ध	रे	नि	म	प	ग
6.	म	नि	प	रे	स	ग	ध
7.	ग	स	नि	ध	म	रे	प

Hindustani Notation System

There are two systems in existence for notation for both the fields — Vocal and Instrumental — introduced by the great wizards of Hindustani Music, namely Pandit Vishnu Digamber Paluskar and Pandit Vishnu Narayan Bhatkhande. In this book Pandit Vishnu Narayan Bhatkande's notation system has been adopted. Our traditional music is purely a practical art and it can only be learnt from a *guru* (teacher). The notation can only give a sketchy idea of the composition but the finer points of a *rāga* need to be learned at the feet of a *guru*. Many scholars have tried and are still trying to evolve a new system of notation so that we can have a foolproof notation system. But, as of now we are yet to come across such a precise system which can be accepted in general.

1.	Sign of lower octave (*mandra saptak*)	....	*Ni*	*Dha*	*Pa*
2.	Sign of upper octave (*tār saptak*)	....	*Sa*	*Re*	*Ga*
3.	Sign of flattened notes (*komal svara*)	....	*<u>Ga</u>*	<u>Dha</u>	*<u>Ni</u>*
4.	Sign of augmented fourth (*tīvra ma*)	....	*M̍a*		
5.	Sign of pulling (*mīṇḍ*)	....	*SaGa*		
6.	Sign of four or five notes in one beat	....	*SaReGaMa*		
7.	Sign of *krintan* (to be played in one stroke)	....	(*S*) means *ReSaNiSa* (*P*) means *DhaPaMaPa*		
8.	Sign of *kan* (use of corresponding note in one stroke)	....	*Ni* *Sa*	*Re* *Ga*	
9.	Sign of gap (where there is no stroke)	....	*Sa—*	*—Re*	
10.	Sign of *chikarī* (last two strings)	....	*S — — —* *D r r r*		
11.	Sign of accent on a particular note	....	*SaRe, Ga, Re GaMa,* or GaMa *Pa, Ga —Ma,*		

12. Notes (*sargam*) for the purpose of notation writing *S* instead of *Sa*, *R* instead of *Re*, etc.

13. Sign of half-beat .... S— SR, G— GM
    (in half beat *Ra* becomes *r*) Ds rd, Ds rd

14. Sign of *tāl* .... + means *SAM*
    (of *tīn tāl*)

    2 means second *tālī* (5th beat)
    O means *khālī* (9th beat)
    3 means third *tālī* (13th beat)

In a cycle of sixteen beats you have three *tālī*s (clappings): the first on the *SAM*, the second on the 5th beat and the third is on the 13th beat. There is no *tālī* on the 9th beat.

A diagram of *TĪN TĀL*, to show the movement of the cycle is given below:

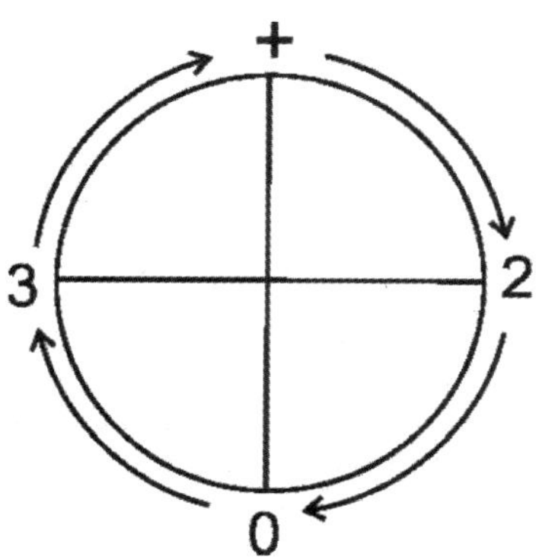

This shows the cycle of (16 beats) *tīn tāl* showing four different signs of *tīn tāl*, i.e. SAM(+), *dūsrī tālī* (2), *Khālī* (0) & *Tīsrī Tālī* (3).

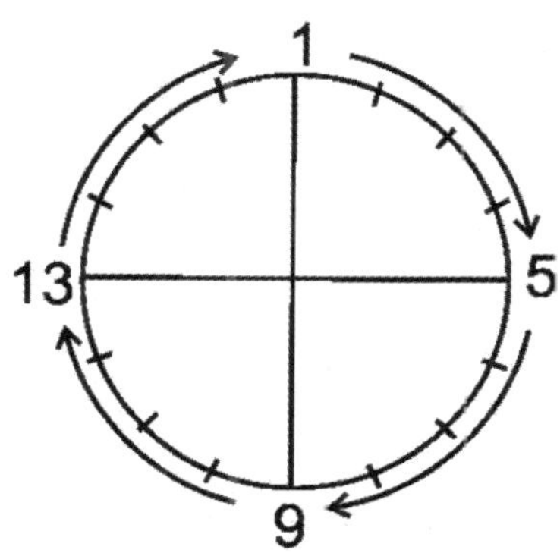

This shows the division of the cycle of 16 beats (*tīn tāl*).

The *bol* of *tablā* as played:

+	2
DHA *DHIN DHIN DHA*	*DHA DHIN DHIN DHA*
0	3
DHA TIN TIN TA	*TA DHIN DHIN DHA*

Note: The cycle is equally divided into four sections and it is a must that a player should come to the *SAM* after improvizations; all these syllables are quite alike to the sound produced on *tablā* and it has no meaning whatsoever.

Different Stroke Patterns (bols)

	S	R	G	M	P	D	N	S
1.	*da*	*ra*	*da*	*ra*	*da*	*ra*	*da*	*ra*
2.	*da*	*dir*	*da*	*ra*	*da*	*dir*	*da*	*ra*
3.	*dir*	*dir*	*dir*	*dir*	*dir*	*dir*	*dir*	*dir*
4.	*da*	*ra*	*dir*	*dir*	*da*	*ra*	*dir*	*dir*
5.	*daS*	*rda,*	*daS*	*rda,*	*daS*	*rda,*	*daS*	*rda*
6.	*dir*	*da*	*daS*	*r,da*	*dir*	*da*	*daS*	*r,da*
7.	*da*	*dir*	*dir*	*dir*	*daS*	*r,da*	*S,r*	*da*

Explanation of Some Basic Terminology of Indian Music

Nāda: Broadly speaking, *nāda* means the sound. According to the Sanskrit grammar, *'Na'* means the vital force (*prāṇa*) and *'Da'* is the fire (*agni*). The word *nāda* is made with these two syllables. *Nāda* signifies the consequence of interaction between the vital force and the fire, which becomes the consciousness of sound.

According to Mataṅga, the word *nāda* is derived from the root *nad* which means "to sound".

Nāda is of two types — (a) *anāhata* (unmanifest) *nāda*, which can only be heard after deep meditation and (b) *āhata* (manifest) *nāda*, which has the power of entertaining the masses, and it can be produced by the vocal chords which serve as a means of enjoyment for the one who produces it and also for the one who listens it.

In music, only *āhata nāda* is used and the notes are produced through it.

Śruti: In music the *āhata nāda* can be differentiated into 22 graces, which can be heard. They are called *śruti*s. According to some scholars, the 22 *śruti*s can be produced with the help of 22 upper *nādī*s, each of the heart, the throat and the cerebrum.

*Śruti*s are known as microtones. In our music, *śruti*s are numbered as 22 in one octave. They are known in relation with consonance of fourth, fifth and third. For example, the intervals of thirteen, nine, seven and six *śruti*s between the two notes are always consonants and our music follows this basic rule.

Svara: *Svara*s (notes) arise out of the *śruti*s. In one octave, *svara*s are mainly considered as seven, viz. *ṣaḍja* (Sa), *ṛṣabha* (Re), *gandhāra* (Ga), *madhyama* (Ma), *pañchama* (Pa), *dhaivata* (Dha) and *niṣāda* (Ni).

According to Śārṅgadeva, that which comes immediately after *śruti*, creates a sound that resonates with power, and delights the listener's mind by itself is called *svara*.

The *śruti* itself is a *svara* only when it stands on its own and is being played in a particular sound. Every musical composition is based on this very sound called *svara*.

Pakaṛ: *Pakaṛ* literally means to seize. In music, it means the main phrase of the *rāga* which can distinctly identify its character. This phrase is made to seize the soul of the *rāga* in the shortest possible notes.

Chalan: *Chalan* means the various types of note patterns by which a *rāga* is delineated in different ways. In *chalan*, one can have a fairly good amount of *rūpa* (picture) of a *rāga*.

Saptak: Literal meaning of *saptak* is seven notes, but in Western music it is termed as an octave adding the *sa* after the seventh note in the higher octave. Although in Western music, octave means "*c d e f g a b c*". But in Indian music, the concept of *saptak* is from"*c*" to "*b*", i.e. seven notes. The word *saptak* means *Sa, Re, Ga, Ma, Pa, Dha,* and *Ni*. Students of music often make mistake by taking eight notes as *Sa Re Ga Ma Pa Dha Ni Sa* and calling it a *saptak*. Though for the theoretical purposes, *saptak* stands for the group of seven notes, but as far as the practical aspects are concerned, the upper "*Sa*" is taken in the ascending order also, to have the feeling of completion. Our "*Sa*" can be on any frequency and in relation to "*Sa*", other notes acquire their respective places.

In *sitār*, technically speaking, there are $2^1/_2$ octaves, starting from *mandra* (lower) leading to *madhya* (middle) and *tar* (upper) octaves. But in some instruments, one can have $3^1/_2$ octaves adding one more *laraj kā tar* (lower bass tonic).

Jāti: *Jāti* signifies the number of notes or *svara*s used in the ascending and descending orders. It is mainly of three types — *sampūrṇa* — using seven notes, *ṣaḍava* — omitting one note, i.e. usage of six notes only, and *auḍava* — omitting two notes, i.e. applying just five notes in a *rāga*. By combining these three, total number of *jāti*s come to nine:

1. *Sampūrṇa-sampūrṇa* — Using all the seven notes in the ascending as well as in the descending orders, e.g. Rāga Yaman.
2. *Sampūrṇa-ṣaḍava* — A *rāga* containing seven notes in the ascending order and six notes or *svara*s in the descending order.
3. *Sampūrṇa-auḍava* — A *rāga* taking all the seven *svara*s in the ascending order but omitting two notes in the descending order.
4. *Ṣaḍava-sampūrṇa* — A *rāga* omitting one note in the ascending order but using all the seven notes in the descending order, e.g. Rāga Jaunpurī.
5. *Ṣaḍava-ṣaḍava* — A *rāga* avoiding one note both in the ascending order and the descending orders, e.g. Rāga

Marwā.

6. *Ṣaḍava-auḍava* — A *rāga* that contains six notes in the ascending order and five notes in the descending order.
7. *Auḍava-sampūrṇa* — A *rāga* taking five notes in the ascending order and seven notes in the descending order, e.g. Rāga Deś.
8. *Auḍava-ṣaḍava* — A *rāga* that contains five notes in the ascending order and six notes in the descending order, e.g. Rāga Rāgeśrī.
9. *Auḍava-auḍava* — A *rāga* that avoids two notes both in the ascending and the descending orders, e.g. Rāga Bhūpālī.

Rāga — *Rāga* is the central and the most prominent feature of Indian classical music. The peculiar order of sounds which is decorated or beautified with *svara* and *varṇa* (practical act of singing) and is pleasing to the listeners is called a *rāga*.

There are certain rules that determine the character of a *rāga*. First of all, no melodic structure can have less than five notes and the nature of the notes should be definite, i.e. natural, flat or sharp. *Ṣaḍja* is never omitted in a *rāga* and along with it both *madhyam* or *pañcham* cannot be avoided simultaneously, because our music essentially rotates around the concept of the cycle of fourth and fifth. Out of the notes used in a *rāga*, one note gets extra importance which is technically known as *vādī* and the note which has a second place in a *rāga* is known as *samvādī*. Rest of the *svara*s are all known as *anuvādī*.

Every *rāga* has an initial phrase which determines its individuality so that it can easily be distinguished from rest of the *rāga*s. Certain characteristic phrases are used to give a *rāga* its character which is known as *chalan* of a *rāga*. Besides this, every *rāga* is performed at a specific time. In Indian classical music, while playing a *rāga*, the tonic (base note) never changes.

Thāṭ — *Thāṭ* is a systematic grouping of seven notes chosen from the octave. Any note (*śuddha, komal* or *tīvra*) is used in a *thāṭ* for the purpose of grouping the *rāgas*. The main difference between *rāga* and *thāṭ* is that *rāga* is a melodic theme which pleases the mind of a listener, whereas *thāṭ* is sequence of seven notes without any aesthetic appeal in it. There are ten *thāṭs* devised by Pandit Bhatkhande and generally accepted by the Hindustani Music system to classify the *rāgas*. They are as follows:

	Thāṭ				Svara			
1.	Kalyāṇ	*Sa*	*Re*	*Ga*	*Ma*	*Pa*	*Dha*	*Ni*
2.	Bilāwal	*Sa*	*Re*	*Ga*	*Ma*	*Pa*	*Dha*	*Ni*
3.	Khamāj	*Sa*	*Re*	*Ga*	*Ma*	*Pa*	*Dha*	*Ni*
4.	Bhairav	*Sa*	*Re*	*Ga*	*Ma*	*Pa*	*Dha*	*Ni*
5.	Pūrvī	*Sa*	*Re*	*Ga*	*Ma*	*Pa*	*Dha*	*Ni*
6.	Marwā	*Sa*	*Re*	*Ga*	*Ma*	*Pa*	*Dha*	*Ni*
7.	Kāfī	*Sa*	*Re*	*Ga*	*Ma*	*Pa*	*Dha*	*Ni*
8.	Āsāvarī	*Sa*	*Re*	*Ga*	*Ma*	*Pa*	*Dha*	*Ni*
9.	Bhairavī	*Sa*	*Re*	*Ga*	*Ma*	*Pa*	*Dha*	*Ni*
10.	Toḍī	*Sa*	*Re*	*Ga*	*Ma*	*Pa*	*Dha*	*Ni*

Mīṇḍ — *Mīṇḍ* is an integral part of Indian classical music and this word is mostly attributed to instrumental music, though the same can also be used in vocal music. In fact, *mīṇḍ* is taken in the slowest possible manner by deflecting the string (by pulling it). It is a part of ornamentation. There are two types of *mīṇḍ* . One is *sīdhī* (forward) *mīṇḍ* and the other is *ulṭī* (backward) *mīṇḍ*. The following plates will show the technique of playing the *mīṇḍ* while keeping the fingers in their correct position.

SĪDHĪ MĪṆḌ (FORWARD MOVEMENT)

1.

N	S	R	G	M	P	D	N
NS	SR	RG	GM	MP	PD	DN	NS

2.

S	R	G	M
SRRG	RGGM	GMMP	MPPD

3.

S	R	G	M	P	D
SRG	RGM	GMP	MPD	PDN	DNS

4.

S	R	G	M
SRGRS	RGMGR	GMPMG	MPDPM

5.

S	R	G	M
SRGM	RGMP	GMPD	MPDN

6.

S	R	G
SRGM, MGRS	RGMP, PMGR	GMPD, DPMG

ULṬĪ MĪṆḌ (BACKWARD MOVEMENT)

1.

S	R	G	M	P	D	N
RS	GR	MG	PM	DP	ND	SN

2.

S	R	G	M
GRS	MGR	PMG	DPM

OTHER VARIETIES OF MĪṆḌ

1.

S	R	G	M
SG, GS	RM, MR	GP, PG	MD, DM

2.

S	R	G
SGM, MGS	RMP, PMR	GPD, DPG

Technique of Playing Mīṇḍ

Position of the finger after pulling from *komal "Ni"* to *"Sa"*.

Position of the first finger after pulling from *tīvra "Ma"* to *"Pa"* with one finger.

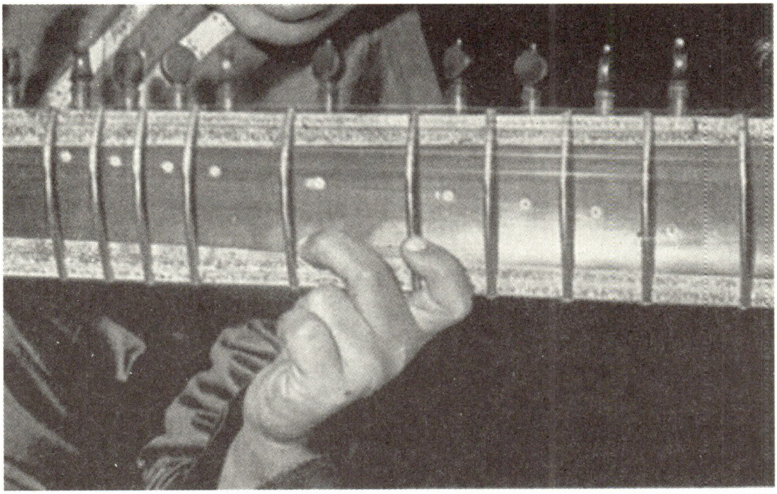

Same technique but here it is pulled fom "*Pa*" to "*Ni*", observe the effect on other fingers.

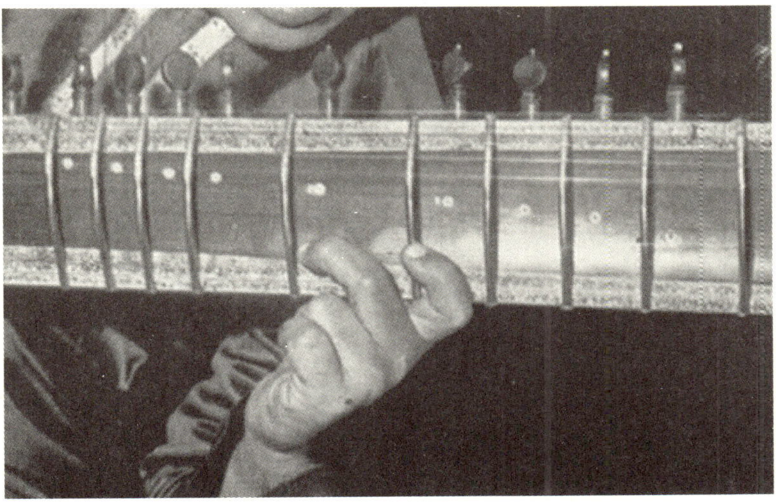

In this picture it is pulled from "*Re*" to "*Pa*" (four notes).

Tiā — A phrase which is repeated thrice is called *tiā*. A mere repetition of a single phrase thrice does not make it complete, unless after repetition it comes to the first beat of a cycle, i.e. "*SAM*".

Tiā is a mere division of certain beats in a cycle. It has nothing to do with a *rāga* as *rāga* has nothing to do with a *tāl*. Confusion prevails that certain *rāga*s must be played in certain *tāl*s, which is not correct. The division of beats can be simple or highly intricate and mathematical too. As such a *tiā* can be played in any *rāga* and the artiste chooses the notes of the respective *rāga*, while playing the *tiā*. The same *tiā* can be played in some other *rāga*, if the notes of that particular *rāga* are used in such a manner, so that the impression of the *rāga* does not get spoilt and the character is also maintained.

Here are few examples of simple *tiā*s, which can fit into all the *rāga*s by the artiste. The following *tiā*s are all set to *tīntāl*. These *tiā*s can either be played in *masit khanī gat* (slow tempo) or in *razā khanī gat* (fast tempo). *Masit khanī gat*s are played in a slow tempo whereas the *razā khanī gat*s are played in speeds two to four times faster than that of *masit khanī gat*s. So, the *tiā* which will be played within four beats in *masit khanī gat* would possibly take eight, twelve or sixteen beats of (fast) *tīntāl*. In order to make it clear for the students of *sitār*, the examples of *tiā*s given below are meant for *razā khanī gat*, i.e. a faster movement and in the same manner as stated earlier. The following *tiā*s are all set to *tīntāl*-cycle of sixteen beats. Different *tiā*s are started from different beats to show that a *tiā* can be of any number of beats.

Sr. no.	1 X	2	3	4	5 2	6	7	8	9 0	10	11	12	13 3	14	15	16
I.													GM	P,G	MP,	GM
II.												GM	P—,	GM	P—,	GM
III.									G—	—M	P—,	G—	—M	P—,	G—	—M
IV.									GM	PM	P—,	GM	PM	P—,	GM	PM
V.									—G	—M	P—,	—G	—M	P—,	—G	—M
VI.						GM	PG	—M	P—,	GM	PG	—M	P—,	GM	PG	—M
VII.						PM	—G	—M	P—,	PM	—G	—M	—P,	PM	—G	—M
VIII.	GM	PM	PG	—M	P—	- -,	GM	PM	PG	—M	P—	- -,	GM	PM	PG	—M

Note: We are taking only three notes just to show that these three notes can make many *tiās*. These divisions can again be composed in a new variety, adding a gap of half a beat to any number of beats in between these three notes, but *tiās* are always attractive to listen to and play if they are played possibly and preferably within one or two cycles. If a *tiā* is repeated three times which becomes nine times in actuality of a single phrase; it is then called a *chakradār tiā*.

Jhālā — *Jhālā* is the most fascinating part of *sitār* playing and most of the people like it because of its sound, music, and rhythmic patterns, which make the most interesting and attractive part of music. It takes the music to its climax. In the West, the listeners enjoy the *jhālā* portion the most.

The *jhālā* is traditionally played after *ālāp* and *joṛ*. In fact, the *joṛ* is a combination of note-patterns, stroke-patterns and *jhālā*. Any traditional player who follows the *bīn aṅg* (style) would play *jhālā* in the last part of *joṛ*. There are three stages of *ālāp*, i.e. *vilambit, madh* and *drut*. Unfortunately, the latest trend in the announcement of an instrumental performance, especially in the All India Radio, has created lot of confusion about *jhālā*. My *guru* was very much against such announcements where it says "*ālāp, joṛ* and *jhālā*".

Jhālā is also played within the framework of a cycle, after the *razā khanī gat* (fast composition). Traditionally, the compositions of *jhālā* are played in *tīntāl*, a cycle of 16 beats, and it is divided into four sections, for example:

+		2		0		3
S— — —	|	*S*— — —	|	*S*— — —	|	*S*— — —

It means "*Sa*" is played on the main string and three strokes played on the last two-three strings are known as *chikarī*.

So, sixteeen beats are divided into four sections, as it has been said earlier, but can also be divided in the following manner:

	1	2	3	4	5	6	7	8	9	10	11	12	13	14	15	16
	X				2				0				3			
1.	S	—	—	—	S	—	—	—	S	—	—	—	S	—	—	—
2.	S	—	—	—	S	—	S	—	S	—	—	—	S	—	—	—
3.	S	—	—	—	S	—	—	—	S	—	S	—	S	—	S	—
4.	S	—	—	S	—	—	S	—	S	—	—	S	—	—	S	—
5.	S	—	—	S	—	—	S	—	—	S	—	—	S	—	S	—
6.	S	—	S	—	S	—	S	—	S	—	—	—	S	—	—	—
7.	S	S	—	—	S	S	—	—	S	S	—	—	S	S	—	—
8.	S	S	S	—	S	S	S	—	S	S	S	—	S	S	S	—
9.	S	—	—	S	—	—	S	—	S	—	—	—	S	—	S	—
10.	S	—	—	—	—	S	—	—	—	—	S	—	—	S	—	—

(difficult one)

These sixteen beats can be divided according to the artistic ability of the player but patterns 1 to 5 are very common and be played regularly.

There is another type of *jhālā*, known as *ṭhoṅk jhālā*, which is once again played by the *bīn-kāras*. Here are some examples:

	1	2	3	4	5	6	7	8	9	10	11	12	13	14	15	16
	X				2				0				3			
1	—	S	—	—	—	S	—	—	—	S	—	—	—	S	—	—
2	—	S	S	—	—	S	S	—	—	S	S	—	—	S	S	—

Note: "*da* and *ra*" mean strokes and only *R* means *chikarī*. *Chikarī* is played with the help of the last two or three strings. In this notation system, the sign of *chikarī* is shown as — or after the respective note, i.e. S — means SA with three *chikarīs*. In this type of *jhālā*, the stress is mainly on *chikarī* strings.

Different Note Patterns (Set on 7 *bols* showed earlier)

Sr. no.	1 X	2	3	4	5 2	6	7	8	9 0	10	11	12	13 3	14	15	16
1.	S da	R ra	G da	M ra	P da	D ra	N da	S ra	S da	N ra	D da	P ra	M da	G ra	R da	S ra
2.	S da	RR dir	G da	M ra	P da	DD dir	N da	S ra	S da	NN dir	D da	P ra	M da	GG dir	R da	S ra
3.	S da	R ra	GG dir	MM dir	P da	D ra	NN dir	SS dir	S da	N ra	DD dir	PP dir	M da	G ra	RR dir	SS dir
4.	SS dir	RR dir	GG dir	MM dir	PP dir	DD dir	NN dir	SS dir	SS dir	NN dir	DD dir	PP dir	MM dir	GG dir	RR dir	SS dir
5.	S— daऽ	S,R r,da	G— daऽ	G,M r,da	P— daऽ	P,D r,da	N— daऽ	N, S r,da	S— daऽ	S,N r,da	D— daऽ	D,P r,da	M— daऽ	M,G r,da	R— daऽ	R,S r,da
6.	SS dir	R da	G— daऽ	G,M r,da	PP dir	D da	N— daऽ	N,S r,da	SS dir	N da	D— daऽ	D,P r,da	MM dir	G da	R— daऽ	R,S r,da
7.	S da	RR dir	GG dir	MM dir	P— daऽ	P,D r,da	—D, ऽr,	N da	S da	NN dir	DD dir	PP dir	M— daऽ	M,G r,da	—G, ऽr,	R da

Note: The above note patterns are meant to be played in *tīntāl*, i.e. cycle of sixteen beats for practice.

Concept of Rasa in Music

The concept of *rasa was* introduced by Bharata in his treatise *Nāṭyaśāstra* (fourth century BCE). *Rasa* is an awareness of the totality of the emotional situation and its experience is absolute. There are said to be nine *rasa*s corresponding to nine emotional conditions: *śr̥ṅgāra* (erotic), *hāsya* (humorous), *karuṇa* (pathetic), *raudra* (furious), *vīra* (valorous), *bhayaṅkara* (fearful), *bībhatsa* (odious), *adbhuta* (wonderous) and finally *śānta* (peaceful) which was later on added by Abhinavagupta.

It has been the practice from the earlier days to relate these *rasa*s to music which has no valid explanation whatsoever. *Rasa*s like *bībhatsa, adbhuta, hāsya,* etc. cannot be justified in our music. *Rasa*s without the visual effects, especially some of those which are mentioned here, have no significance in our music.

The connotation of *rasa* has four different meanings, namely, (i) sap, juice, (ii) flavour, relish, (iii) delight and (iv) quintessence. In art, all these four ideas are included in the word *rasa*. It is very difficult to communicate or translate the word *rasa* into any other languages. It is a kind of feeling, a peculiar relish and delight. In Sanskrit, scholars have interpreted the concept of *rasa* in relation to *kāvya* or poetry. But all the details, as said earlier, cannot be attributed to music; only a few are applicable. In order to experience *rasa* in music, the emotional factor plays a vital role. In practical life, one may experience sorrow but when this aspect is expressed in a *rāga*, like Pīlū, which is full of *karuṇa rasa*, it gives us a fine and wonderful aesthetic feeling and joy. To appreciate *rasa*, one must have certain amount of detachment from the rigidity of life and must be out to dwell in the universal experience. To understand and appreciate *rasa* one must "become one" within himself which may be termed as *tanmayatā*. The musician must be *tanmaya* to the core or one with the *rasa bhāva* in order to express the *rasa*. It is an experience beyond this materialistic world and that is why it has also been called *alaukika*, a transcendental experience; a prerequisite for expressing the essence of notes, for example *komal ṛṣabha* gives a feeling of sadness, *tīvra gandhāra* gives a feeling of cheerfullness, freshness and pleasant atmosphere, etc.

There is an important link between *rasa* and *rāga*.

> The beauty and vitality of every melodic type are expressed as a cumulative effect of the *bhāva*s of *rasa* which is inherent in it. Many melodic types are classified as *rāginī*s or the feminine types, and some as *rāga*s or the masculine types on the basis of *bhāva*. In order to further the views, *rāginī*s are categorized as *nāyikā*s and *rāga*s as *nāyaka*s. But certainly the lamentation of a woman or a loud laughter or an expression of joy cannot be the music. They only become music when all these notes are combined in a regulated form and put into a particular theme in a particular context. The theory of *rasa* can be applied in its proper context where poetry plays its vital part, with a little bit of acting with a proper surrounding. The musical notes itself are not enough to express and create its desired effect . . . and that is what we may call *saguṇa upāsanā* in music. We give music a certain definite visible shape and worship it. Otherwise music, pure and simple, is the expression of the soul.

In our *rāga*s, there is no place for provocative sentiments of laughter, fury, terror, or dismay, as mentioned earlier. Only due to these reasons, our *rāga*s manifest only four sentiments, i.e. pathetic, erotic, heroic and aesthetic. In instrumental music, it is rather difficult to express these sentiments but in case of vocal music it is much more easier because of its poetry. The main object of the exposition of *rāga*s is to create an aesthetic sentiment (*rasa-siddhi*) and often these sentiments are marred by applications of *tān*s, *gamaka*s, *murkī*s, etc. at a wrong place without realizing the mood of the *rāga*. Although, according to Bharata, there were eight *rasa*s which could be applied to *nāṭya-saṅgīt*, but at present we come across *śānta rasa*, *bhakti rasa*, etc. which have been accepted today. It may be observed that some *rāga*s do not appeal to some and some other *rāga*s do appeal and give an aesthetic feeling as a result of a particular expression of the melodic structure and its application of notes. So it is very difficult to define a particular note or a *rāga* that can give a feeling of a particular *rasa*. It is the total effect of the exposition which creates the atmosphere and the aesthetic sense in the mind of the listeners. Embellishments are meant to enhance the mood of the *rāga* and its particular *bhāva*, and its proper application in proper place helps create the *rūpa* (picture) and *rasa* of the *rāga*.

North Indian Tāl System (Time-measure)

Although it is mentioned in *Saṅgīta Ratnākara* that there are at least 120 examples of *tāl*s but most of them are not in practice today. In the modern days, we come across only 20 to 25 *tāl*s and others are not being played. It is said that *sitār khanī ṭhekā (bol*s) were specially meant for a particular composition to be played in *sitār* only, but unfortunately that too is forgotten today.

Here I will also include some rare *tāl*s which are still played in the eastern part of India with *kīrtan*, a rare folk form of Bengal.

1. *Tīntāl:*		4+4+4+4	=16 beats (already shown earlier)				
2. *Cautāl:*		2+2+2+2+2+2	= 12 beats cycle				
	Dha Dha X	Dhin Ta 0	Kit Dha 2	Dhin Ta 0	Tita Kata 3	Gadi Gina 4	
3. *Ektāl:*		2+2+2+2+2+2	= 12 beats cycle				
	Dhin Dhin X	Dhage <u>Tirkit</u> 0	Tu Na 2	Kat Ta 0	Dhage <u>Tirkit</u> 3	Dhin Na 4	
4. *Adachautāl:*		2+2+2+2+2+2+2	=14 beats cycle				
	Dhin <u>Tirkit</u> X	Dhin Na 2	Tu Na 0	Kat Ta 3	Tirkit Dhin 0	Na Dhin 4	Dhin Na 0
5. *Dhamār:*		5+2+3+4	= 14 beats cycle				
	Ka Dhi Ta Dhi Ta X		Dha — 2	Ga Ti Ta 0	Ti Ta Ta — 3		
6. *Sūltāl:*		2+2+2+2+2	= 10 beats cycle				
	Dha Dha X	Din Ta 0	Kit Dha 2	Tita Kata 3	Gadi Gena 0		
7. *Jhamptāl or Jhampa:*		2+3+2+3	= 10 beats cycle				

Contd. . .

	Dhin Na X	Dhin Dhin Na 2	Tin Na 0	Dhin Dhin Na 3
8.	*Rūpak:*	3+2+2		= 7 beats cycle
	Tin Tin Na X	Dhin Na 2	Dhin Na 3	
9.	*Tīvra or Teoda:*	3+2+2		=7 beats cycle
	Dha Din Ta X	Tita Kata 2	Gadi Gena 3	
10.	*Dādrā:*	3+3		= 6 beats cycle
	Dha Dhin Na X	Dha Ti Na 0		
11.	*Dīpchaṇḍī:*	3+4+3+4		=14 beats cycle
	Dha Din — X	Dha Ge Tin — 2	Ta Tin — 0	Dha Ge Dhin — 3

SOME TĀLS USED IN KĪRTAN OF BENGAL

12.	*Chañchupuṭa tāl:*	4+4	= 8 beats cycle
	Gedda Gighi Neda Ghi X	Gedda Gighi Neta Khi 2	

Contd. . .

13 *Baḍā (long) Daśkośī:* 4+4+4+4+4+8 = 28 beats cycle

Ta X	—	Tin	Da	Tin	Da	Khi	Khi	Takhi
Ta 2	—	Tin	Da	Tin	Da	Khi	Khi	Takhi
Tata 3		Tata	Khikhi	Gurgurgurgur				
Ta 4	—	Tin	Da	Tin	Da	Khikhi	Takhi	

14. *Teot Tāl (short):* 3+3+4+4 =14 beats cycle

TA X	—	Ta	—	—	Gurgurgurgur		
Tat 2	Tete	Tete	Khiti	Nak 3	Dadhe	Ida	Dhei

15. *Lofa (long) Tāl:* 3+3+3+3 = 12 beats cycle

Did X	da	jhee	Nak 2	tete	tete
Khe	Ta	Jha	Ta	—	Gurgurgurgur

Note : These *tāl*s are mostly played on *śrīkhol*, a percussion instrument specially played with *kīrtan*s of Bengal.

Rāgas Suitable for Instrumental Music

In Indian classical music there are more than 1,000 *rāga*s which are known only to the connoisseurs of music. In the earlier days, a great master was known for his knowledge of music and his command over *rāga*s and it was expected that a maestro must have a command over 100 *rāga*s. Today there are some great masters who are capable of executing more than 100 *rāga*s including the *bandiśe*s. In fact, the contribution of Bhatkhande in documenting more than 1,000 compositions is a constant companion to the artistes and students of today. Vocal music has an advantage over instrumental music as the fact remains that there are no such books available where the students could learn the compositions as documented by Bhatkhande.

In vocal music, *sthāyī* and *antarā*, must be there in a composition and this composition gives an advantage to the students of music to have a wider knowledge of the subject. But unfortunately this is not the case with the instrumental music. As a result the instrumental performers have a lesser importance in the modern times compared to the vocal experts. Even in the education system this aspect is also neglected. The instrumental students are the major sufferers. I have seen during my forty years of teaching at the faculty of music in University of Delhi that the instrumental students have always been handicapped for resources.

If you take *rāga*s like Dev-Gandhāra, Śukla-Bilāwal, Śuddh-Kalyāṇ, Darbārī-Kānhṛā, Megh, Gorakh-Kalyāṇ, etc. these are extremely difficult for an instrumental student to perform, whereas a vocal student can do it better in comparison. Although many great vocal maestros used to perform very limited *rāga*s but in case of instrumental performers the expectations are much higher.

In order to have a better understanding of the subject and in the interest of instrumental students there is a need to have a documentation on the compositions in instrumental music like Bhatkhande's monumental work (*Kramik Pustak Mālikā*).

I am still trying to document at least 100 compositions with the support of 100 vocal compositions so that the students of instrumental music are not subjected to psychological harassment. Some *rāga*s which are the favourites of the instrumental music performers are given below for the ready reference where one can perform with better command rather than trying to play Jait-Kalyāṇ or Gorakh-Kalyāṇ, which are favourite *rāga*s of the vocalists. *Rāga*s that suit instrumental music are given below:

1. Yaman
2. Bihāg
3. Bhūpāl
4. Kāfī
5. Bāgeśrī
6. Rāgeśrī
7. Jhiñjhoṭi
8. Mālkauṅs
9. Bahār
10. Sahānā;
11. Śyām-Kalyāṇ
12. Durgā
13. Deś
14. Tilak-Kāmode
15. Māru-Bihāg
16. Marwā
17. Purya-Dhaneśrī
18. Sohinī
19. Miāṅ-Malhār
20. Śaṅkara
21. Paṭdīp
22. Śrī
23. Purya
24. Madhuwantī and
25. Kāmode.

Note: All the above mentioned *rāga*s are played in the evening or at night.

1. Toḍī	:	morning
2. Jaunpurī	:	morning
3. Bilāwal	:	morning
4. Alahiya-Bilāwal	:	morning
5. Bhaṭiyār	:	morning
6. Bhairav	:	morning
7. Gurjarī-Toḍī	:	morning
8. Ahīr-Bhairav	:	morning
9. Bhairbī	:	morning
10. Guṇkalī	:	morning
11. Bairāgī	:	morning
12. Vasant-Mukharī	:	morning
13. Naṭ-Bhairab	:	morning
14. Multānī	:	afternoon
15. Śudh-Sāraṅg	:	afternoon
16. Vr̥ndābanī-Sāraṅg	:	afternoon
17. Gauḍ-Sāraṅg	:	afternoon

Note: These are some of the *rāga*s which normally any instrumentalist would love to play. The vocalist would also love to sing some of these *rāga*s.

It is given to understand that all *rāga*s are not suitable to play for all musicians. That is why the *rāga*s mentioned above are generally favourites of the instrumental music performers although some of the *rāga*s mentioned here are the favourites of vocal musicians also.

The idea to bring out this aspect is to highlight the problems of instrumental music performers, *vis-à-vis* vocal performers. There are various logical reasons behind this but one should always try to understand and analyze the problems and find out answers based on reasons.

4

Rāga and Tāl

Tablā is a combination of two pieces i.e. *bāyāṅ* (which is placed on the left hand side) and *dāyāṅ* (placed on the right hand side). This is the standard way of playing and placing *tablā*. But in some cases it is the opposite for left hand players.

If you take one part out, either the bass or the treble, then it cannot be called a *tablā*. Unlike *pakhāwaj* or *mṛdaṅgam,* we come across both bass and treble together in shape, whereas in *tablā* the shape is different and distinctly separate in two pieces.

When we talk of *tablā,* in any music profession, the dictum is that it must have both treble and bass pieces. *Tablā* and *pakhāwaj* are the most popular north Indian drums and *mṛdaṅgam* is the most popular drum of the south. *Pakhāwaj* is played in accompaniment with Dhrupad singing and *tablā* is played with instrumental music or vocal music or in any other kind of music. *Pakhāwaj* is played with Dhrupad as a solo, and also to the accompaniment with *rudra vīṇā.*

There is a misconception amongst many listeners particularly those who have not sufficient exposure to Indian music that *rāga* is co-related to *tāl,* which is not correct. A *tāl* can be played with any *rāga* and a *rāga* can be played in any *tāl*. *Rāga* is a concept other than a melody concept but a *tāl* is a concept of keeping the rhythm cycle and pace. The function of the *tablā* or *tāl* is to maintain the cycle of particular rhythmic structure, whereas, the concept of *rāga*s is based upon the melodic structure. Many a time, I have come across several queries of listeners who think that a particular *rāga* must be played in a particular *tāl*, which is not correct. A *rāga* must essentially have the following attributes:

Ascending (*ārohī*), descending (*avarohī*) and notes (*svara*), *vādī* (dominant notes) *samvādī* (next to dominant notes) catch notes (*pakaṛ*). The term *pakaṛ* signifies some combinations of notes which are always predetermined once a *rāga* is decided. These combinations of notes give an outline on the *rāga* and this outline must meet the grammatical formation, because a *rāga* cannot be established without following the grammar.

Great masters have been extremely particular on the aspect of the grammar of a *rāga*. I have seen some of them who used to scan a note (*svara*) in such a meticulous way that they could bring out the essence of a *rāga* by applying a particular *śruti* of a note (*svara*) and they could easily bring out the essence of another *rāga* applying a different *śruti* on the same note (*svara*). Such was their mastery over a *rāga* for applying its grammar in its purest form that they could easily produce a glimpse of five to ten *rāga*s by applying only one note (*svara*).

This is something so intricate which is extremely difficult to comprehend and understand in the modern times. I say it with all humility, because today everyone expects a quick result and as a consequence no one has the time to scan a note which should be applicable to a particular *rāga*. I recall one incident which took place way back in the year 1948. Once I went to learn *sitār* as usual from my *gurujī* Ustad Mushtaq Ali Khan Sahib in Calcutta. Suddenly the famous Dhrupad singer Pandit Tansen Pandey (Husainuddin Dagar), of Ḍāgar Gharānā, who used to visit my *gurujī* frequently, arrived there. After having some informal chat Pandey suddenly started discussing 'Rāga Śrī' which is a very rich *rāga*, and the discussion went on from the morning till the afternoon. It was around 3:00 p.m. when my *gurujī*'s wife called him for lunch. Both of them had forgotten the lunch and we students, were also so much involved in the discussion that we too did not think about the lunch even for a moment.

It may be quite surprising for many artistes and students of art today that a discussion went on for five hours just only for one note (*svara*) and its application on a particular *rāga* which was the *komal ṛṣabh* (D-flat) of Rāga Śrī The second flattened note *re komal* has a tremendous impact on the *rāga* and the discussion went on that subject alone. In how many ways the same note could be applied without having to initiate or imitate the colour of any other *rāga* having the same note.

When I think of it today I realize such learned discussions are quite rare indeed. But those moments are still haunting my mind only to realize, how invaluable moments I have witnessed those days. The beauty of treating a particular note in different *rāga*s lies in its proper application called *svara lagāv*, which is the essence of the Indian *rāga* system.

Music being a performing art, the aspects of application of a *svara* is so predominant that the ambience of a *rāga* entirely depends on it. As I have said earlier, one note has various colours and shades and it is only relevant when a *rāga* is chosen and the shade and colour automatically come to the mind of a performer as taught by his/her *guru*. Because this is such an intricate matter that it cannot be explained in writing or in any other way that is why it is called *guru-mukhī-vidyā*. India is the land of Vedas and the chanting of the Veda, which we hear today, is being carried on from *guru* to *śiṣya* from down the ages. Such is the beauty of the Indian classical music that it is always a matter of great pleasure to listen and learn the intricacies of applications of a *svara* of various *rāga*s. This aspect is rather difficult to be understood by the Western ears. As I have said earlier, a scale having a *komal ṛṣabh* (D-flat) will have various *rāga*s, e.g. Rāgeśrī, Pūrbī, Purya-Dhanāśrī, Marwā, Purya, Basant, Gaurī, etc.

All these *rāga*s are to be played in the evening or at night, as per the grammar of Indian classical music. But there are many other *rāga*s having the same flattened note, that is *komal re* (D-flat) which are used in the morning also. The interesting feature however is that the same note is used as per the mood and the expression of the *rāga*s and the basic principle is the proper application. This can only be learnt from a learned *guru*. Our age-old tradition is known as *guru-śiṣya paramparā* (*maukhik paramparā*). That is why Indian classical music can never be learnt without the help of a *guru*. Any book on the performing arts is incomplete without the guidance of a *guru*, whereas a book on the theoretical aspect, can perhaps be well understood without the guidance of a *guru*.

As I have said earlier, *rāga* is a melodic concept and it has nothing to do with the *tāl* system but the music cannot be complete without *tāl*. That is why the accepted terminology of music is the combination of three statics/practice:

1. *Svara* (note),
2. *Pada* (text), and
3. *Laya* (rhythm) and *tāl*.

So when we talk of music we must understand that it must have the three basics: a note, text and rhythm, and this can be applied to vocal music as well. As for the second aspect, *pada* (text) it can be pronounced vocally, but in case of instrumentalists *pada* is substituted by *bol*s (strokes). A *bol* is the instrumental expression of the text in a composition. A vocalist can sing a *rāga* with certain text prescribed for the particular *rāga* and an instrumentalist, while playing the same *rāga* will play a instrumental composition keeping the spirit of the *rāga* in its truest form. But there are some instrumentalists who play the same vocal composition often take the help of the stroke patterns. They thus try to keep the spirit of vocal *bandiś* much closer; for example if we have to sing a line *bhaj hari nām* now, how can one produce these words *bhaj hari nām* in *sitār* or *sarod*? It is only possible with the help of strokes and musical patterns.

When coming to *laya* and *tāl* we have to understand that *tāl* is a major cycle. As we have many *rāga*s so we have many *tāl*s too; but when we sing and play a *rāga* we may not start with *tāl* at all because *rāga* is a melodic concept but when we start singing or playing a composition (*bandiś*) then we must have a *tāl*. It is interesting to know that the word "composition" is translated from the technical name *bandiś*. But it is also interesting to know that the word "composition" is used in the Western music in a different context. It had happened with me during my tours abroad that the music-loving audiences were many times confused with the word "composition". Those who know the Western music know what exactly I am trying to explain in comparison to our *bandiś*.

We have different *rāga*s for 24 hours and for all seasons having their moods and expressions as Śāstras. It has been mentioned earlier that *rāga*s must have their mood and *rasa* (we have already dealt with a chapter on *rasa* earlier). Even *rāga*s of the season have their own mood, whether it is winter, monsoon, summer or autumn. In the year 1982, I recorded 24 hours *rāga*s to prove that our *rāga*s are based on time theory. This is another unique aspect of Indian classical music, where we have *rāga*s for every hour and for every occasion. That is why various *rasa*s are mentioned in Śāstras while giving the details of any *rāga*.

Tāl

Speaking of *Tāl* it is another technical aspect which is unique in its form but there still is one common factor, i.e. *laya* whether it is in Indian or Western music it has its same principle. *Laya* is a tempo and it is universally accepted that there are only three kinds of basic tempos, e.g. slow *(vilambit laya)*, medium *(madhya laya)* and fast *(drut laya)*. So the universally accepted divisions are mentioned here, but if one tries to go much slower than the slow tempo then it can be called as *ati-vilambit* and if anyone can go faster than prescribed then it is *ati-drut laya*. So *laya* is a tempo which is defined in three categories as mentioned above. Therefore, when we start performing the b*andiś* (composition) after the exposition of *rāga* (*ālāp*), we start from *vilambit laya* then gradually pass on to *madhya laya* and finally go to the *drut laya,* which is the climax. In fact, during my tours abroad many listeners, after listening the recital, came and asked me, "Why don't we start from the climax", because they liked the speed. Indian classical music is based on spiritualism and the purpose (goal) is to reach a certain spiritual height, in order to attain *mokṣa*.

Our music is not merely for pleasure, but also to elevate the listeners to a spiritual height where they can have their blissful experience of life.

As we have many *rāga*s in Indian classical music we have many *tāl*s also. The *tāl*s not only keep a steady flow of the music but also add the beauty and colour of the performance. *Tāl*'s role is to keep the cycle and maintain the beats and these beats also play a vital role in making the music complete.

What is most interesting is that the master of *tāl* while playing also creates various kinds of *tāl*s within the framework of *tāl* system and the instrumentalist or the vocalist whom he is accompanying also enjoys the intricate patterns woven within the set *tāl*. It is very much interesting to note here that any first beat of a cycle (*tāl*) is known as *SAM* and a *bandiś* must have its starting point and *SAM* which is repeated a number of times. But when both the players come to the first beat (*sam*) with a bang together it creates a heavenly atmosphere. We must not forget that in Western music it is "composition" and not *bandiś*. It is all written from the beginning to the end but in Indian music a "composition" is only set with cycle system (*tāl*) which is repeated a number of times within a performance and it is not written from the beginning to the end. On the other hand it is based on a cycle (*tāl*) which could be of any number of beats, e.g. 16, 14, 12, 10, 8, 7, 6. There could be many more beats but as I have said, the first beat of any *tāl* (cycle) is called *SAM* and it is so important that any musician practising Indian classical music must come to *SAM* after creating varieties of musical ideas. I have given a brief idea of different *tāls* where it is explained in a simpler manner so that it can be easily understood by a common man, when you talk of *tāl*. It consists of various kinds of syllables (*bols*) and that is the language of *tablā*.

As we have *SA; RE; GA; MA; PA; DHA; NI* in vocal music, which are the notes applied in music, similarly the syllables (*bols*), i.e. *DHA; NA; TE; RE; KE; TE; DHIN; TA; GADI; GHINE* etc. (*bols*) are used in *tablā*. I have given illustrations of fifteen *tāls* by giving their syllables and divisions (see Chapter 3 pp. 47-49). It may be interesting to note that certain *bols* are pronounced in a poetic manner like *KA; TA; TE; TA; TRIK* (short form of *tirakita*); *KAT*. In these syllables (*bols*) *TA* is sometimes pronounced as in English "T" and sometimes like Spanish *TA* and that is why I have always been advocating that music is a *guru-mukhī vidyā* and a book may only be a stepping stone but we must learn the art from a *guru;* even how to pronounce *TE* and *TA*. I have also tried to give an idea of how the fingers are placed on *tablā* according to its *bols* (see illustrations on next page). Here again the pictures may not give you the actual pronunciation of the *bols*, but my attempt is to convey it in such a manner, so that it becomes interesting even for a layman. Anyone who would like to advance in learning in order to have a better knowledge of *tablā* must go to a teacher or a *guru*. Let us also remember that whatever I have tried to convey herein may not be fully correct as the issue concerns a performing art!

In Indian classical music, as one may be aware, there are 108 *tāls* as mentioned in the thirteeth-century treatise *Saṅgīta Ratnākara*. *Tāl* is an important factor in our music which binds us with a rhythm and other factors like *sam* and *khālī*. Normally, in a recital, we come across *tāls* which are gerenally used by the performers of today. But it is interesting to note that there is another attempt being made to play even those *tāls* which are otherwise played normally such as $8^1/2$, $10^1/2$, $11^1/2$, etc. But *tāls* like *tīntāl, ektāl,*

Different Ways of Placing Fingers on Tablā

DHA

DHA

DHIN

DHIN

NA

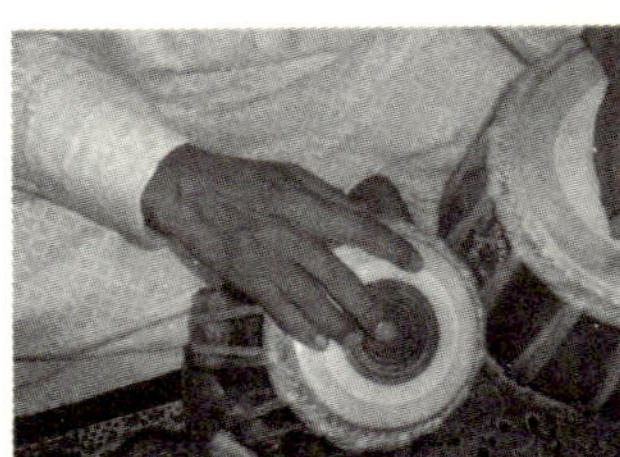

NA

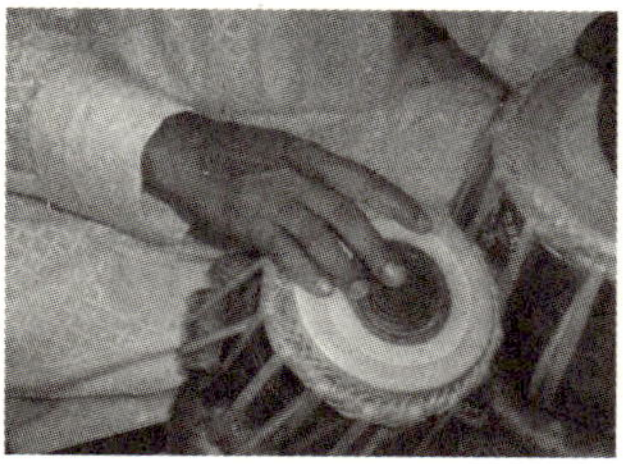

NA

TE

RE

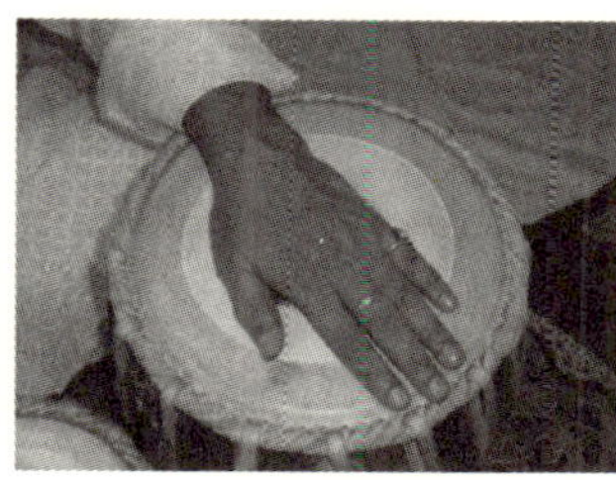

KE

KE

KAT

KAT & TA same

KAT & TA same

TE

TE of *TIRAKITE*

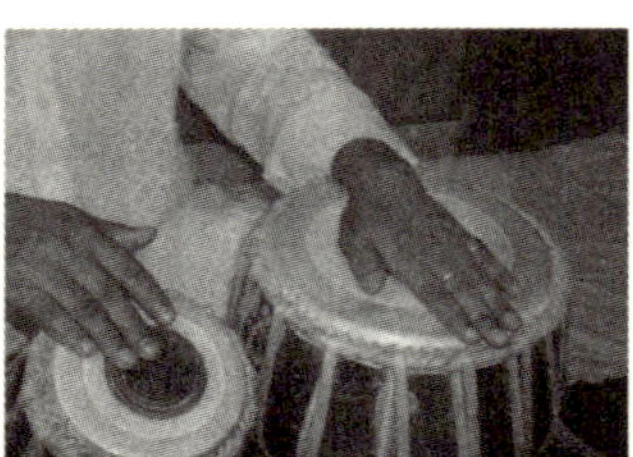

TE of *TIRAKITE*

TE last syllable of *TIRAKITA*

DHI

DHI

GA

GA

DI

DI

GHE

NE

NE

THUN

THUN

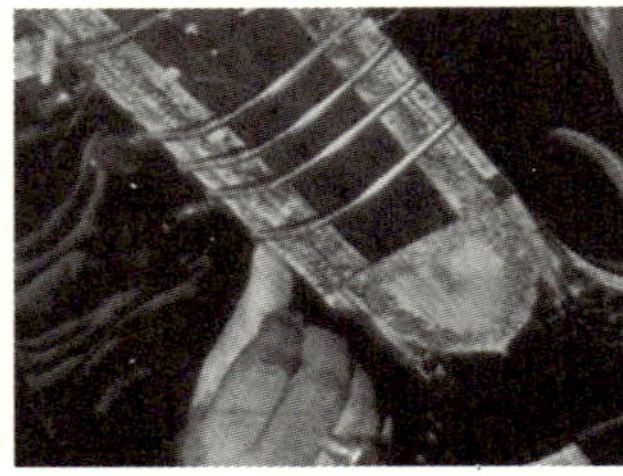

TUN

DHI

RE

DHI

DHI

DHI of *DHITE*

TE of *DHITE*

TE of *DHITE*

TE of *DHITE*

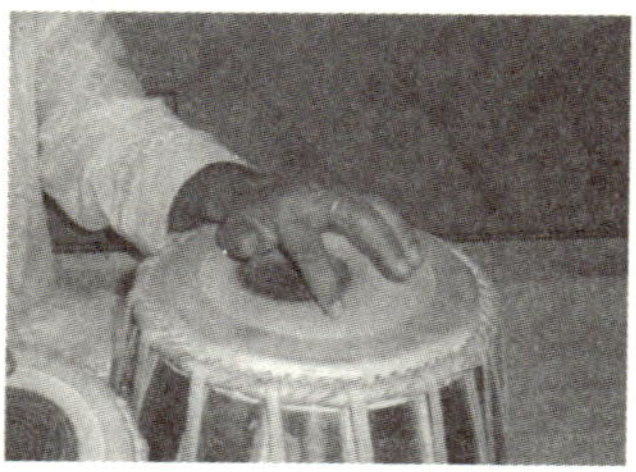

GHE

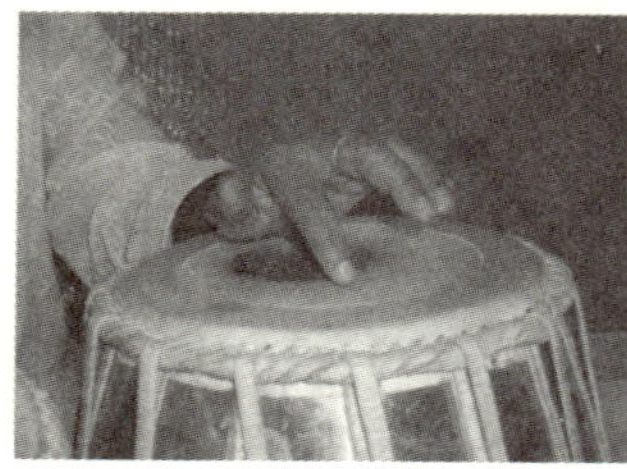

GHE

GE of *GHEGE*

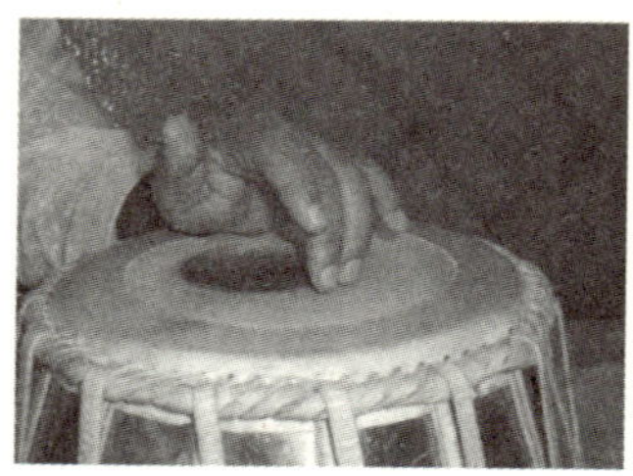

GE of *GHEGE*

TIN

TIN

dhamār, chautāl, sultāl, jhaptāl, rūpak, kaharwā, etc. are mostly used by the musicians both in vocal and instrumental music. There are established *gharānā*s on *tablā* known as *bāj* like Delhi, Ajrara, Banaras, Lucknow, Punjab, etc.

There are many *gharānā*s who have enriched their *gharānā* and their style of playing over a period of time. Today the involvement of accompaniment has assumed great importance and attraction which was not the case in the nineteenth century. We must also know that each *tāl* has its own division (bar), e.g. a *tāl* having a 10 beat cycle and known as *jhaptāl* has four sections viz. 1 2/3 4 5/6 7/ 8 9 10. In this *tāl* the first section having two beats starts from *SAM* (1 and 2) (1st beat of any cycle); then we come to the second section having three beats (3, 4 and 5), then comes the third section which is known as *khālī* written as zero (6 and 7). While writing the *khālī,* which comes on the sixth beat of third section and the final section comes on the eighth beat which gives another beat that signifies as the third beat which means 8th, 9th, 10th. Here we have to understand that in this *tāl* we have ten beats divided into four sections. A clap on the first beat, i.e. *SAM* and the second beat on second section that is on third *mātrā,* and on the third section which starts from the sixth *mātrā* there is no *tāl,* so there will be zero. And again, on the fourth section the third *tālī* will come on the eighth beat or *mātrā* so the division of *jhaptāl* is; 1 2/3 4 5/6 7/ 8 9 10.

Example is given below:

X		2			0		3		
Dhi	*Na*	*Dhi*	*Dhi*	*Na*	*Ti*	*Na*	*Dhi*	*Dhi*	*Na*
1	2	3	4	5	6	7	8	9	10

Now, to keep the beat in a traditional way, in terms of clapping, we have to clap three times and no clapping in between on the sixth beat as shown above. So, when writing a *tāl* we have to write on top of the *bol,* the *tālī*s and *khālī*. When we recite the *ṭhekā* of *jhaptāl* or any *tāl,* we normally keep the cycle by clapping as mentioned above. If we have to play this *tāl* it has its own rhythmic *laya* that means you cannot just recite 10 syllables, although this is a part of mathematics. As we have to keep the cycle in mind and always come to *SAM*, which is the first beat of a *Tāl*, it will not give the feeling of a *tāl* which is divided into four sections. Thus the division of ten in a way may be counted as 1 2 / 1 2 3 / 1 2 / 1 2 3. It may be interesting to note that *tīntāl* having sixteen beats can be played in any speed without disturbing the musicality whereas in other *tāls* it is not possible to play in any speed.

I will give an example of one *tāl*, that is (*tīntāl*); *tīntāl* is often called by the great masters as the king of all *tāls*. Now, that I have given a brief illustration of this *tāl*; in fact, this is such a common and popular *tāl* in north Indian music (which is very close to *ādi tāl* of Carnatic music), it has sixteen beats divided into four sections (4+4+4+4) and 1st beat known as *SAM* and the 9th beat known as *khālī*. Each *tāl* having a cycle of its own, e.g. 16, 12, 10, 6, etc. have their own name and identity of keeping own sections (as the 1st beat of any *tāl* in a cycle is known as *sam*, similarly each *tāl* having its *khālī* also). Thus a *tāl* must have its *tālī* and *khālī* depending on its own divisions.

The *dādrā-tāl* often sounds like the waltz of the Western music. So the system of cycling is like beats going round in a clock-wise motion and as soon as the last beat of any *tāl* ends, then one has to be ready for the *SAM*; e.g. if you are playing a cycle of six beats (*dādrā-tāl*) then after the count of six you will be ready to come to an end and each *tāl* is divided into different sessions which is given in the chapter on *tāl*. So a cycle of six beats is divided into two sections as a cycle of sixteen beats is divided into four. Here again, we must remember that each *tāl* can be played in any *laya* (tempo). But I strongly feel that each *tāl* has its own character and tempo, and if we stretch it too far, either making it too slow or too fast, then the essence will be completely lost; for example if we play the *dādrā-tāl*, which is by nature of a medium tempo, too fast then the beauty and nature of the *tāl* will be completely lost. Consider we are watching a Western ballroom dancing, witnessing the dance in a waltz style (rhythm), the music and the tempo automatically make the dancing more enjoyable, and if we want to double the tempo of the same dancing, it will neither be enjoyed nor be appreciated either by the dancer or the viewers. But in case of *tīntāl* it can be sung or played in a very slow tempo or it can be played in a very fast tempo, and that is why, it is called the king of all *tāl*s and no other *tāl* has this particular edge or advantage. As an exception *ektāl* also has the same advantage of playing in any tempo.

We must remember that all popular *tāl*s mentioned about are meant for Khayāl, and instrumental music, but when we come to the richest form of Indian classical music, i.e. Dhrupad, it is generally forbidden.

There are, no doubt, certain *tāl*s which are played with Dhrupad such as *chautāl*, *dhamār* and *sadrā* or *sulfaktā*.

The nature of Dhrupad singing is always majestic and compositions are always sung in the slow tempo and not in the fast tempo.

Although there are some exceptions when we come across a composition sung in *sultāl*, which some masters sing in faster movement, it will be interesting to note that a *rāga* has nothing to do with *tāl*. *Rāga* is a concept and is the soul of Indian classical music. To understand *rāga* we have to visualize a concept. It is a melodic expression based on a grammar and the grammar being followed strictly while performing with the following principles, which must be there in a *rāga*.

a. It must have a minimum of notes (*svaras*);

b. It has to have ascending and descending orders (*āroha-avroha*);

c *Vādī* — dominant note in a scale; *samvādī* second dominant notes which play the part of the relation of 1-3; 1-4; 1-5. If the first notes are *vādī* then the 4th or the 5th notes in a scale must be *samvādī*, and some people call it *vād* — *samvād*;

d. Time theory — in Hindustani music we are still following the time theory in the presentation of a *rāga*, whereas in Karnatic Music this is no more applicable. Each *rāga* is earmarked for its time of presentation depending on the notes applied. The general belief is that any *rāga* having a combination of *svara*s is meant for the morning depending on its application. But the same combination of *svara*s may be used in the evening melody by somewhat changing its colour and shade. There are many *rāga*s not having any *komal* (flat note) *svara*s, these are generally meant for the afternoon and evening time. But this principle cannot be observed at random. Such is the beauty, concept and depth of the time theory.

e. *Jāti* means the nature of the *rāga* in its ascending and descending order; *jāti* signifies how many notes should be taken in *ārohī* and *avarohī*. It determines the nature of a *rāga* and there can be five notes in *ārohī* and seven notes in *avarohī*. If five notes are taken then it is called *auḍava*, in case of six notes it is called *ṣaḍava*, and with seven notes it is called *sampūrṇa*. And finally, the *pakaṛ* by which a *rāga* can be performed as it guides in the formation of the *rāga* by applying notes in a particular order. It may be straight, or back and forth or even in a zig-zag way. While performing a *rāga* we have to remember that we have to apply the notes in a particular way in a particular *rāga*. It is quite interesting in Indian classical music that each *rāga* has its own character and each note has its own way of applications.

The same note of a scale may have a different shade and colour in another *rāga*, which is a highly intricate subject to discuss be it the second note (Re) or third note (Ga) or any other note. For that matter it will not be the same in two different *rāga*s. A note used in the morning and the same note when used in the evening has different nature of application and that is why Indian music is so settled that a note (*svara*) if applied in a correct way can create heaven on earth. My revered *gurujī* Ustad Mushtaq Ali Khan Sahib's widely known quotation on our music is worth mentioning as follows:

svara hai īśvar, laya hai jnān,
tan hī path hai, rūpa hai dhyān.

A *rāga* is a melodic structure combining the above-mentioned factors where one tries to bring out the essence of it. That is why the connoisseurs of music can make out from the first notes sung or played by the performer. As a result when some artistes are performing it is evident from the first phrase what *rāga* he or she is going to sing. This was the tradition in earlier days. As I have said earlier, the same note, while performing a different *rāga,* will have a different application. Thus, one note in our music can have various shades and colours by which the character of a *rāga* is determined. A popular *rāga* having a third minor note *komal ga* can easily bring out the difference of the Rāga Darbārī or Rāga Pīlū. That is why the application plays a major role in our *rāga* system. We also remember that while keeping the grammar of a *rāga* in mind each artiste has his/her own way of presentation where the style of presentation may be different but should strictly follow the grammatical order of marking. That is why the word "tradition" plays a vital role in Indian classical music. When we play *rāga* from the traditional point of view, we strictly follow the rules, but when we do not follow the traditional pattern we often go off the track. I say this because in the modern times the performers are trying to innovate various ways of applications but they have got to follow the tradition and the laws of the *rāga*. Here again, a word called *tālīm* is extremely important and relevant which means a rigorous training taken at the feet of *guru*. Then only one is known as "Tālīm-i-Afta" and those who have been trained under the *guru* and are having sound *tālīm* are respected by the connoisseurs of music. Even today, our time theory is another landmark factor which is unique in the world of music. Morning *rāga*s having the same notes may be sung in the evening or at midnight but interestingly enough these two *rāga*s are entirely different in nature, for example, "Rāga Jaunpurī (morning *rāga*)", "Rāga Darbārī", "Kānhrā"(night *rāga*) are completely different in nature but the scale is one and the same. This is the beauty of Indian classical music.

5

Gharānā

Gharānā is a word which is very much used by the musicians although there has never been any serious research on the subject. This situation certainly raises some complex questions. If we try to understand its meaning then our mind immediately goes back to those luminaries who have contributed enough to our music. Then the question as to how their principles are to be followed comes to our mind, which need to be studied in depth and understood properly. If we try to analyze the musical term *gharānā* in other art forms it is more widely known as school. In case of painting this term is used very extensively. *Gharānā* in music relates to family and tradition. For example, we talk of the style of singing of Banāras Bāj or Punjab Bāj but here we seldom use the word *gharānā*. We normally say Pūrab or Punjab style in which Pūrab signifies Banāras or Lucknow, especially when we talk of Ṭhumrī style of singing, and Punjab *aṅg* takes us to the western India, Lahore, Multān, etc.

The age-old system of *guru-śiṣya paramparā* is partly responsible in carrying on the style of its own. It is the process but the art in the specialized form is transferred from one generation to the other. When we talk of *gharānā* we mainly think of vocal aspect, but from the history of Tānsen's heredity we come across *gharānā* as the form of instrumental music as well.

Here we will not discuss the voice culture which is meant for vocal tradition but we will lay special emphasis on the instrumental music. An application of a *rāga* and its composition clearly gives the picture of a traditional music in a particular style which is accepted as an individual style and which must maintain its continuity. A distinctive style of music or school is carried on by our age-old *guru-śiṣya paramparā* system. Thus the distinctive style is maintained and carried on further. That is how our traditional music and its originality has survived throughout the ages. Even if the same style is carried on by another generation it will be still known as the same *gharānā,* carried on by the age-old *guru-śiṣya paramparā* system. In the modern times *gharānā*s are fast losing their importance and identity because of the technical advancement and mechanical reproductions. As a result, the restraints of purity are fast losing their ground. In the olden days a *śiṣya* was supposed to blindly follow the *guru* and was not allowed to listen to others' style. As a result the *śiṣya* had to follow his *guru* hundred per cent (blindly) and reproduce the music as the *guru* wanted. Even a *gharānā* was identified with his laws of developing a *rāga* and the different sections of *bandiś*. Today a student is exposed to various styles of singing due to technical advansments and is not strictly following the tradition of his *guru* as the *guru* wants. As a result the wider exposure students are influenced by listening various styles of music from different media and mechanical reproductions in vogue.

Today it is difficult to identify a singer who is yet to make his name in the field of music or which school he belongs to. To conclude I would like to mention some of the leading *gharānā*s which have contributed immensely to the growth and development of our classical music. Apart from the Seniā Gharānā the branches that flourished and became famous as a school by themselves include Gwālior Gharānā, Āgrā Gharānā, Jaipur Gharānā, Bhīṇḍī Bazaar Gharānā, Atraulī Gharānā, Lucknow Gharānā, Mathurā Gharānā, Rāmpur Gharānā, Sahaswān Gharānā, Khurjā Gharānā, Indore Gharānā, Kirānā Gharānā, Paṭiyālā Gharānā, Sham Chaurasi Gharānā, etc.

Gharānā means a school of music which gives a definite style of presentation depending on the name of it. Like *sitār*, as I have said earlier, the origin of all *gharānā*s is regarded to be the Gharānā Tānsen, which is widely known as Seniā Gharānā. From Seniā

Gharānā, we come across various branches from the line of a son or daughter, a brief family tree of Tānsen relating to *rabāb* and *bīn*. Later on they were known as either the *rabābī*s or *bīnkār*s *gharānā*. In relation to *sitār* we come across a definite style invented by Masit Sen (Khan) who was a great *sitār* player of the Tānsen family and till now his style is known as *masit khanī bāj* which is played by all *sitār* players in *vilambit laya* (slow tempo). Later on, Gulam Razā Khan introduced the composition (*bandiś*) in fast tempo the (*drut laya*) *razā khanī gat*. In trying to concentrate on the topic of *sitār* only certain other related factors of instrumental music are not taken in this particular topic. We have to know that *sitār* is the most popular musical instrument in Indian classical music. There have been many *gharānā*s that became popular and many great masters of the nineteenth and twentieth centuries have contributed in its development and growth.

It is very unfortunate that traditional instruments like *bīn*, *rabāb* and *sur-śṛṅgār* are not heard today. Now while referring to a *gharānā* of a *sitār* player, we have to go back once again to Masit Khan, son of Rajras Khan and the grandson of Karim Sen. There have been many great instrumentalists from the Seniā Gharānā. Some names worth mentioning are Zafar Khan, A.R. Khan, Basat Khan, etc.

Some Seniā *sitār* players later on came to Jaipur and were known as Jaipur Seniā Gharānā. From Jaipur Seniā saw the emergence of great players like Amrit Sen, Barkat-Ulla Khan, etc.

Yet another family of Bīnkār went to Indore and came to be known as Indore Bīnkār Gharānā which was founded by Bande Ali Khan during the reign of Allauddin Khalji. Later on in *sitār* a *gharānā* in the name of Ustad Imdad Khan Sahib was founded by Ustad Sahabdad Hussain Khan followed by Maihar Seniā Gharānā founded by Ustad Saddu Khan. In the art of *sitār* playing and the great masters who made it popular, we also come across another *gharānā* called Bishnupur Gharānā founded by Ustad Bahadur Khan, the famous *sitār* player. Bhagwan Chandra

Das was also instrumental in establishing a *gharānā* which was founded by Haricharan Das Swami. During the same period we come across the emergence of Banāras Gharānā founded by Pandit Dayal Mishra and Darbhaṅgā Gharānā by Rameshwer Pathak and Ram Govind Pathak. In the later part of the nineteenth century emerged Pandit Jiten Bhattacharya's Gharānā that was founded by Ram Kamal Shiromani, and later on popularized by Pandit Laxman Bhattacharya. Ustad Yusuf Ali Khan, the great *sitāriyā* of Lucknow, also made his style quite popular and this *gharānā* was founded by his father Ustad Bahadur Hussain Khan. Later on Ustad Ilyas Khan of this Lucknow Gharānā made his *gharānā* further popular. It is interesting to note that in the earlier part of the twentieth century the Seniā Gharānā's Ustad Barkat-Ullah Khan, who was a student of Amrit Sen, was regarded as the leading *sitār* player of Jaipur Seniā Gharānā. Ustad Ashique Ali Khan, the father of Ustad Mushtaq Ali Khan, had the good fortune of learning at the feet of Ustad Barkat-Ullah Khan, who played *sitār* with 17 frets. The technique of playing *sitār* with 17 frets, was continuing from the time of Masit Khan, the originator of *masit khanī* style (*bāj*). A unique feature of this tradition is that it represents an uninterrupted line of *sitār* players of nine generations who have been playing *sitār* with 17 frets till date. This is the only *gharānā* in the art of *sitār* playing in the Seniā Tradition, whereas other *gharānā*s have been playing *sitār* with 19 or 20 frets today.

While mentioning Imdad Khanī Gharānā (Iṭāwā Gharānā), we have to remember the great contributors of this *gharānā* like Ustad Imdad Khan, Ustad Inayat Khan, Ustad Wahid Khan and Ustad Vilayat Hussain Khan. Recently, the followers of Ustad Vilayat Khan have started naming this *gharānā* as Vilāyat Khanī Gharānā. The contribution of Ustad Vilayat Khan in the art of *sitār* playing can never be forgotten or overlooked. The influence of his style was so powerful that many players of today are following the style with a particular string arrangement on *sitār* (*gandhār-pañcham*). There was also another branch of *gharānā* of instrumental music as Indore Bīnkār Gharānā which was popularized by the great players of *vīṇā*, Ustad Babu Khan, Majid Khan or Rajab Ali Khan and Mohammad Khan.

Ustad Halim Zafar Khan, the *sitār* maestro, is the follower of this very *gharānā*. The contribution of Hamiduddin Khan, Jamaluddin Khan, Aabid Hussain Khan and Sajjad Hussain Khan, cannot be ignored in popularizing this *gharānā*. The late Shri Bimal Mukherjee, a famous sitār player (who was the student of Abid Hussain Khan of Indore), not only made a name for himself but also for this *gharānā*.

Another *gharānā* which later came to be known as Seniā Maihar Gharānā was popularized by Ustad Allauddin Khan and Ustad Aayat Ali Khan, both the great *sarod* maestros. Ustad Allauddin Khan was a the disciple of great Seniā *bīn* player Ustad Wazir Khan. Ustad Ali Akbar Khan and Shrimati Annapurna Devi were the son and daughter of Ustad Allauddin Khan. Although Ali Akbar Khan was a *sarod* player, Annapurna made a name in the art of *surbahār* playing. Ustad Bahadur Khan son of Aayat Ali Khan also made a good contribution to the art of *sarod* playing. Bishnupur Gharānā has also contributed in the development of Indian classical music which was popularized by famous musicians like Pandit Kshetra Mohan Goswami, Anant Lal Bandopadhyay, Gopeshar Bandopadyay, Krishan K.C. Dey, Girijashankar Chakraborti, Tarapad Chakraborti, Gokul Nag, and his son Manilal Nag, who added to the name and fame of this *gharānā* as a *sitār* player.

In Banāras Gharānā contributions of Chote Ram Das, Amulya Charan Mukherjee and Laxmi Parshad made the *gharānā* richer with their performance and in case of Darbhaṅgā *Gharānā*, the famous *sitār* player Rameshwar Pathak made it richer and later on the son of Ram Govind Pathak, Pandit Balram Pathak, made this *gharānā* quite significant with his inimitable style having 22 frets. Special mention may also be made of Pandit Laxman Bhattacharya who in his early 40s in the twentieth century brought a new dimension to the art of *sitār* playing. It will be worth mentioning of string system of this *gharānā* that the both sitārists Pandit Rameshwar Pathak and Pandit Laxman Bhattacharya used *laraj* string (lower octave) in their *sitār* along with *kharaj pañcham* (in the lower octave).

We must pay our due regards to the great *sitār* players of the twentieth century, whose names have already been mentioned in the development of *sitār* and the various *gharānā*s. They not only contributed in the development of the different styles but also left an indelible mark in the performing art of *sitār* playing. Although there are many brilliant *sitār* players among the younger generation of today who not only are making their future in *sitār* safe in their hands but are also showcasing as to how the great masters of the twentieth century have changed the trend of *sitār* playing and how they have contributed in the development of the art of *sitār* playing. The exceptionally great contribution of Kanailal, Hiren Roy and Rikhiram is worth mentioning here. As we see the *sitār* today, we must remember that most of the changes in the sound and shape are the contribution of these great manufacturers of *sitār*.

In the middle of the twentieth century we come across some great names of *sitār* players who have changed the mind of the listeners of today. Who could think of a deflation (*mīṇḍ*) of five to six notes on one fret in *sitār* in the nineteenth century. We should not forget the great names like Ustad Inayat Khan, Ustad Yusuf Ali Khan, Ustad Hamid Hussain Khan and Ustad Mushtaq Ali Khan, Pandit Gokul Nag, Pandit Ravi Shankar, Ustad Vilayat Hussain Khan, Pandit Laxman Bhattacharya, Ustad Iliyas Khan and also Pandit Nikhil Banerjee (who was also a student of Ustad Mushtaq Ali Khan for some time) of the early 1940s. Although Pandit Nikhil Banerjee was junior to these great masters but he made a mark as a maestro and continued to contribute and perform till his death. His music was appreciated by the lovers of Indian music because of his aesthetic approach in the development of *rāga*s. The next generation was fortunate in having many brilliant performers and many of them, although they were young, earned a name for themselves in the art of *sitār* playing.

Sitār being the most popular among musical instruments, we come across many brilliant players of *sitār*. As compared to any other musical instruments the style of Pandit Rameshwar Pathak did influence the *sitār* music of the twentieth century but the contribution of Ustad Mushtaq Ali Khan, Pandit Ravi Shankar and Ustad Vilayat Khan changed the entire trend of *sitār* playing, although great players like Ustad Yusuf Ali Khan, Pandit Laxman Bhattacharya, Pandit Gokul Nag and Ustad Halim Jafer Khan also contributed in the growth and development of the art of *sitār* playing which can never be forgotten. The present generation must remember the contribution of these great masters. Today when we come across the brilliant players of this instrument we find the style of Ustad Vilayat Khan is being followed by many players. Ustad Mushtaq Ali Khan Sahib's style of music was quite popular during the 1940s to 1960s and banking on this popularity the next generation of sitārists including his own students made it widely known.

String Arrangements of Sitār

Now we will take up the popular string arrangements of *sitār* as recommended by the master players of this instrument. It may also be noted that the standard gauge of the strings used has also changed in case of *tarab* strings (sympathetic strings). Some have 12 and some have 13 or 14 strings and the gauge size has also changed from lighter gauge to thicker gauge.

At present there are four established string arrangement systems being followed by the players:

1. The standard traditional way of *sitār* string arrangement and tuning of the seven strings are detailed below:
   i. 1st string tuned in (*Ma*) — (4th note: middle octave) (*saptak*) known as *bāj-ke-tār;*
   ii. 2nd string tuned in (*Sa*) — (1st note: middle octave)

known as *joṛ-ke-tār;*

iii. 3rd string tuned in (*Sa*) — (1st note:) known as *joṛ-ke-tār;*

iv. 4th string tuned in (*Pa*) — (5th note: lower octave) known as *kharaj kā tār;*

v. 5th string tuned in (*Pa*) — (5th note: middle octave); steel string;

vi. 6th string tuned in (*Sa*) — (1st note: middle octave); and — *baḍī chikarī;* and

vii. 7th string tuned in (*Sa*) — (1st note: higher octave) last string — *chhoṭī chikarī.*

Note: This system was followed by most of the traditional players.

2. Ustad Inayat Khan, the prominent *sitār* player, used to follow the original string arrangements (traditional way of tuning) of *sitār* having seven strings in the following manner:

   i. 1st string in *Ma* (4th note, middle octave);

   ii. 2nd and 3rd strings in *Sa* (1st note, middle octave) called *joṛ-ke-tār;*

   iii. 4th string in *Pa* (5th note, lower octave);

   iv. 5th string in *Pa* (5th note, middle octave);

   v. 6th string *Sa* (1st note, middle octave); and

   vi. 7th string *Sa* (1st note, higher octave).

   Note: Here one *joṛ-ke-tār* and one *pañcham* are not used, one steel string is used in the third note, i.e. *Ga.*

3. String arrangement of Ustad Mushtaq Ali Khan Sahib is in the same traditional way as follows:

   i. 1st string in *Ma* (4th note, middle octave);

   ii. 2nd and 3rd strings in *Sa* (1st note, middle octave) called *joṛ-ke-tār;*

   iii. 4th string in *Pa* (5th note, lower octave);

   iv. 5th string in *Pa* (5th note, middle octave);

v. 6th string in *Sa* (*baḍī chikarī*) (1st note, middle octave); and

vi. 7th string in *Sa* (1st note, higher octave).

4. Pandit Ravi Shankar's string arrangement:
He has introduced one *laraj-ke-tār* (lower octave — *Sa* and taken out one *joṛ-ke-tār*, the other strings remaining the same.

i. 1st string in *Ma* (4th note) b*āj-ke-tār;*

ii. 2nd string in *Sa* (1st note);

iii. 3rd string in copper *Pa* (lower octave);

iv. 4th string in bronze or copper *Sa* (lower octave) *laraj-ke-tār;*

v. 5th string in steel *Pa* (middle octave);

vi. 6th string in *Sa* (1st note, middle octave); and

vii. 7th string in *Sa* (1st note, higher octave).

Note: *Ma, Sa* — middle octave, *Pa* — lower octave, *Sa* — lower *laraj*, *Pa* — steel-middle octave, *Sa Sa* — *baḍī* (middle) and *chhoṭī (tār) chikarī.*

5. String arrangements of Ustad Vilayat Khan:

i. 1st string in *Ma* (4th note, middle octave) b*āj-ke-tār;*

ii. 2nd string in *Sa* (1st note, middle octave)(one *joṛ*);

iii. 3rd string in *Ga* (3rd note, middle octave);

iv. 4th string in *Pa* (5th note, middle octave);

v. 5th string in *Sa* (1st note, middle octave); and

vi. 6th string in *Sa* (1st note, higher octave).

Note: The application of *Ga* (3rd note) and *Pa* (5th note) was introduced by Ustad Vilayat Khan Sahib. In this system there is only one *joṛ-ke-tār* and no *pañcham* of the lower octave. Instead he has introduced one steel string tuned in 3rd note, i.e. *Ga*.

6. Pandit Nikhil Banerjee's string arrangements (he used 8 strings instead of 7):

i. 1st string in *Ma* (4th note) *bāj-ke-tār;*

ii. 2nd string in *Sa* (1st note);

iii. 3rd string in *Pa* — lower octave;

iv. 4th string in *Sa* — lower octave (*laraj*);

v. 5th string in *Ga* (3rd note);

vi. 6th string in *Pa* (5th note);

vii. 7th string in *Sa* (1st note: middle octave); and

viii. 8th string in *Sa* (higher octave).

Note: He has combined both Pandit Ravi Shankar's *laraj-ke-tār* and Ustad Vilayat Khan Sahib's *gandhār* (3rd note) thus making it total eight strings.

7. Pandit Debu Chaudhuri's string arrangements:

i. 1st string in *Ma* (4th note), *bāj-ke-tār;*

ii. 2nd string in *Sa* (1st note), *joṛ-ke-tār;*

iii. 3rd string in *Pa* (5th note, lower octave), *kharaj-ke-tār;*

iv. 4th string in *Pa* (5th note, middle octave), *steel-ke-tār;*

v. 5th string in *Sa* (middle octave), *pehlī-baḍī-chikarī;*

vi. 6th string in *Sa* (middle octave), and *dūsrī-baḍī-chikarī; and*

vii. 7th string in *Sa* (1st note, higher octave),*chhoṭī chikarī.*

6

Instrumental Music in Seniā Gharānā

The name Seniā Gharānā is often used by the masters and the students of Indian music to express their pride, belief and faith in the style of Miāṅ Tānsen, the great legend of Indian music, often called as the father of Indian classical music. A *gharānā* or a school is named only after a great master or a composer who leaves behind a distinct stamp of the style of music or a style which is distinct and different from other styles. It may often be named after a place of birth or sometimes even after a great artiste.

Tānsen was a great Dhrupad singer and his mastery and richness in singing made him the court musician of the Mughal Emperor Akbar and was hailed and respected by most of the musicians of his time. His music had such a pristine purity and had a special way of presentation of a *rāga* that it is being followed with pride and glory even today. He not only composed many a Dhrupad but also gave a new dimension of classical music in preserving our age-old tradition with a firm grip on Dhrupad idioms without deviating from his own tradition. There are many interesting stories about his command and capabilities in music and over *rāgas* which could easily invoke fire or rain with his performance. Such was the power of his music that he had a tremendous followers and even today many of our great masters take pride in associating themselves either as a follower of Tānsen's style/*gharānā* by virtue of having relationship from the line of their ancestors or by our age-old tradition, i.e. *guru-śiṣya paramparā*. The author of the book himself is the follower of this most important tradition though having no direct relationship with the founder but by virtue of having learnt from his *guru*, Ustad Mushtaq Ali Khan Sahib who had the fortune of learning it from his father Ustad Ashique Ali Khan Sahib, who too had no blood relationship with Tānsen, but learnt from his *guru* Āftāb-i-Sitār, Ustad Barkat-Ullah Khan, who was distantly related to Miāṅ Tānsen.

Before we proceed further we must know what is meant by a Seniā Gharānā. My revered *gurujī* Ustad Mushtaq Ali Khan Sahib used to say by naming Seniā or claiming a Seniā doesn't give a "carte blanche" to anyone if they are not following the principles of the Seniā tradition in its true spirit. Today there are very few scholarly musicians living who can prove this aspect of a Seniā style or *bāj*. The word *bāj* is used by the instrumentalists only, and whenever we talk of *bāj* it is clear that we are talking about the style of playing instruments specially *vīṇā, sur-śṛṅgār, rabāb, sur-bahār, sitār, sarod*, etc. There was a time when *vīṇā* was very popular and it was essential that *vīṇā* must follow the principles of Dhrupad. *Vīṇā* or *rudra vīṇā*, accepted as the mother of all instruments, was to accompany Dhrupad singers. Rather it was played along with Dhrupad singing that is why when we listen to a *vīṇā* recital it sounds as if we are listening to a Dhrupad in *vīṇā*. *Vīṇā*, in the earlier days, used to be played with three *mizrāb*s to follow and reproduce the sound of the vocal idioms and *pakhāwaj*. *Pakhāwaj* is the percussion instrument played with Dhrupad singing. Some of the phrases in *pakhāwaj* were reproduced in *vīṇā*. Such as *Da, Ga, Ra, Dagar Da, dra*, etc. Any musician calling himself a Seniā follower must follow and play the instruments in the line of Dhrupad.

Sur-bahār at a later stage became a very popular instrument. It is a parallel of *vīṇā* and it was played in principle of the *vīṇā*, playing along with an accompaniment of *pakhāwaj*. Although *sur-bahār* came into existence at a much later stage but *vīṇā* has its roots embeded deep in the Indian tradition. Even we come across the most popular picture of Goddess Sarasvatī holding *vīṇā* in her hand. It is very difficult, therefore, to specify the period in which this was invented but it is true that *vīṇā* even today represents the true spirit of Dhrupad tradition.

Those who claim to be followers of Seniā tradition must be aware of the fact that the basic principles and techniques of this tradition must be adhered to in their purest form. For example, no Seniā player will play *vīṇā* with *tablā* for accompaniment, similarly, no Seniā singer will sing Dhrupad with *tablā*.

This Seniā tradition has been carried on from the time of the great Masit Sen, the ancestor of Miāṅ Tānsen, who used to play *sitār* with 17 frets only. He was the originator of *masit khanī bāj*, the slow speed or *vilambit laya*, which is being played till today by the majority of instrumentalists in India.

Finally, we must realize that one of the basic requirements of Seniā instrumental tradition is that the emphasis on the composition or *bandiś* will automatically tell you that it is a sad state of affairs today when we are ignoring this aspect of classical music. Our vocal music tradition is still following this aspect in one way or the other. But the present trend in instrumental music and its scenario is changing in such a manner that the importance of traditional *bandiś* is now fast losing its importance which is not a very happy sign for the future of instrumental music in India. The traditional Seniā *bandiś* must have the basic sections as it is still followed in Dhrupad today. We may not be able to follow the Dhrupad style of *bandiś* but we can at least have the basic forms of the *bandiś*, which must have *sthāyī, māñjh* and *antarā*. This was the hallmark of Seniā compositions earlier. Even today some of the *bandiś*es are known as *ṭaksālī* (*ṭaksāl*) *bandiś* which means these had the stamp of recognition like a legal tender has the authority of the government.

In the modern times when we are passing through a sea of alround changes, we must in no case neglect the value of our rich traditions. It is the time old traditions which make us proud of our cultural heritage. And if we are proud of the great Seniā tradition we must try our utmost to retain and revive its true form and character for the benefit of Indian classical music of today and for the sake of posterity.

Seniā Gharānā

If, for any reason, our *gharānā* system has survived through the ages, it is only because of the great devotees of the various art forms and their unalloyed dedication to their discipline; it is because of their unflinching faith and devotion to their styles and their *guru*s. Our arts have survived, evolved and prospered even during the darkest period of our tumultuous history.

Dhrupad is regarded as the oldest and the purest form of our classical tradition and it was first introduced in the court of Rājā Mān Singh of Gwalior towards the end of the sixteenth century and prospered under his patronage. It was later on harnessed further not only for the temple worship but also simultaneously to entertain the courtiers of kings and emperors. During the reign of Emperor Akbar, Dhrupad not only flourished but also reached its peak due to the invaluable contribution of Miāṅ Tānsen.

Here I would now like to give a brief account of Tānsen's tradition and the link which binds his followers even till today in the name of Seniā Gharānā. Unfortunately, we do not have a proper background of the Tānsen family and his own children, as a result we have to accept the references available from the books and finally the teachings of our *gurujī*. In this connection I would like to refer the famous books *Ain–i-Akbarī* by Abul Fazl, *Saṅgīta Sudarśana* by Pandit Sudarshanacharya Shastri (a student of Amrit Sen) and Maharaja Birendra Kishore Roy Choudhary's *Hindustani Sangeete Tansener Sthan*. As my revered *gurujī* has told me and as I have myself gathered some information from various sources, I am trying to give here a brief and short linkage of the Seniā tradition and renowned sitārists who played *sitār* with 17 frets till date.

Guru-śiṣya paramparā chart as told by Ustad Mushtaq Ali Khan to his students from the time of Masit Khan (Sen):

Masit (Sen)
↓
Bahadur Sen (Son)
↓
Sukh Sen (Son)
↓
Rahim Sen (Son)
↓
Amrit Sen (Son)
↓
Barkat-Ullah Khan (Student)
↓
Ashique Ali Khan (Student)
↓
Mushtaq Ali Khan (Son)
↓
Devabrata Chaudhuri (Debu) (Student)
↓
Prateek Chaudhuri (Son)

We also have to note that Tānsen was an accomplished Dhrupad singer but his family and one branch at a later stage started playing *rabāb* and *bīn* (known as Jaipur Seniā). From the sketchy records available of these particular *sitār* players of Seniā Gharānā, Masit Khan (originator of *masit khanī bāj*) emerged as a direct descendant in the twelfth generation. A unique feature of this tradition is that it represents an uninterrupted line of *sitār* players of the ninth generation playing *sitār* with 17 frets till date. This is the only *gharānā* in the art of *sitār* playing of Seniā tradition, whereas others are playing with 19 or 20 frets. Many admirers have asked me why do I follow this old system, I only give one answer that my *gurujī* taught me and told me to hold on hence forth. Even Prateek, my son, also follows the same tradition whereas many of my *guru*'s students have switched on to the 19 or 20 frets for their own convenience.

Rahim Sen was a widely respected *sitār* player and he was the only Seniā *sitār* maestro who gave a new dimension to the art of *sitār* playing and later on his son Amrit Sen (1813-93) with him made such a great impact that he was regarded as the best *sitār* player of his time. His compositions in *masit khanī* style are a rare treat to listen to but hard to learn. The speciality of his style was to use maximum notes in one stroke and maintain the true spirit of the *rāga* known as *śuddh vāṇī*. As Amrit Sen had no child of his own he adopted Barkat-Ullah Khan, because of his talent, and taught him the technique of *sitār* playing in *bīn aṅg* and Dhrupad singing. Dhrupad was a must in the Seniā tradition and as a result every player was well conversant with the Dhrupad *gāyakī* which was always reflected in their performance.

My revered *gurujī* Sangeet Acharya Ustad Mushtaq Ali Khan Sahib, who passed away in the year 1989, was the only torch-bearer of our *gharānā,* which still maintains the tradition of Seniā Style playing *sitār* with 17 frets, while all other *gharānā*s are using 19 or 20 frets on their *sitār* and some of them too are known as Seniā. Since my topic here is based on our *gharānā* and the contribution of my *gurujī,* I would like to restrict my topic within that limit. But this will not, in any way, have any reflection on other famous *gharānā*s. So far as Tānsen's contribution to our music is concerned I would like to mention the role of *rabāb* in addition to Dhrupad which was his forte. He was responsible for giving this instrument a classical status. Tānsen's descendants from the daughter's line were known as *bīnkār*s. Great *rabābiyā*s like Muhammad Ali Khan and Chhajju Khan were responsible for maintaining the tradition and then came the instrument *svar-śṛṅgār*, and the famous Jafar Khan, the brother of Pyaar Khan who not only is said to have invented this instrument but also became synonymous with the tradition of Tānsen and his followers. The late Wazir Khan of Rampur, the *guru* of Ustad Allauddin Khan, and Ustad Hafiz Ali Khan was also a great *svar-śṛṅgār* player of Seniā tradition.

If we have to trace back the history of the *sitār* players' *gharānā* on the basis of scanty records available, we have to refer the name of the great Ustad Masit Khan, the twelfth direct descendant of Tānsen, the originator of *masit khanī bāj* (style and technique of *sitār* playing in slow tempo). Ustad Mushtaq Ali Khan had the fortune of being the disciple of his father Ustad Ashique Ali Khan who had the fortune of having a systematic *tālīm* from his *guru* Āftāb-i-Sitār Ustad Barkat-Ullah Khan, the Great Seniā *sitār* maestro of Jaipur Seniā Style who was a great player of Seniā *masit khanī* style, as well as from his father Ustad Sadiq Ali Khan, the famous Dhrupad singer, a descendant of Nāyak Dhundhu. Two traditionally accepted forms (styles) of instrumental music are known as *masit khanī* and *razā khanī bāj*. Although this style has been accepted by all musicians including *sarod* players though the technique of *sarod* playing is different from that of the *sitār* playing. The style of playing fast compositions underwent many changes but *razā khanī* style dominated them all throughout. In addition to these brilliant styles of Seniā traditions we also come across a style called *feroze khanī gat*, composed by Feroze Khan which normally starts from the seventh beat of *tīntāl* and often goes for more than two *āvartans* including *antarā;* but it is quite interesting to note that even in his superb style the basic stroke patterns of *razā khanī* style was followed in principle. Ustad Amir Khan, the great *sarodiā* in turn, made this style popular and taught many students, amongst them the most popular being the late Radhika Mohan Moitra, the great *sarod* player.

Ustad Ashique Ali Khan, father of Ustad Mushtaq Ali Khan, had the privilege of learning the art of playing *surbahār* with three *mizrābs* (plectrum) from Ustad Waras Ali Khan in *bīn aṅg*. *Ālāp* and *joṛ* were being played in *surbahār* before playing *gat-toḍā* on *sitār* in *masit khanī* or *razā khanī* style. Ustad Mushtaq Ali Khan Sahib always used to mention the name of the fifth *vānī* called *dhandvani* which is named after the great Dhrupad singer of Emperor Shahjahan's court, Nayak Dhundu.

The reason of using three *mizrābs* was the fact that the three principal *bols* (storke patterns) — *DA, GA* and *RA* which the Seniā *bīnkārs* used to play. There is a difference in string arrangement and striking pattern in between *rudra vīṇā* and *surbahār*. Today some artistes play *surbahār* in the technique of playing *sitār* which is not the way as it was traditionally played earlier. Here, I would like to quote my *gurujī* on this instrument and its history. Khan Sahib (my *gurujī*) while giving an interview to *The Telegraph* in Calcutta on 13 July 1985 said:

> Ustad Ghulam Muhammed Khan and his son Ustad Sajjad Muhammed Khan used to stay in Calcutta were famous *surbahār* players, who made this instrument widely popular. It is said that Ustad Imdad Khan and Shri Jnanoda Mukherjee were two of his prominent disciples who made it popular not only in Calcutta but also all over India. The art of playing *surbahār* was based on the principle of *bīn* playing technique and as an accompaniment with *pakhāwaj* as in *vīṇā*. As the *ālāp* was played in purely Dhrupad style the *joṛ* was played along with *pakhāwaj* with *talparan* (some call it *tarparan*). After having played the *tarparan* in *joṛ* the tradition was to play *sitār* after *surbahār*.

My *Gurujī*, in the year 1953, participated in the National Programme on All India Radio (A.I.R.) Delhi and played Rāga Purīyā in *surbahār* followed by *sitār* recital which is still fondly remembered even today by those who had heard it.

7

Composition of Basic Rāgas

In this chapter different compositions of ten basic *rāgas* are given along with their descriptions, *ārohī–avarohī* and *chalan*.

Ārohī–avarohī are meant to guide the scale of the *rāga*. It is not essential to follow the *ārohī* and *avarohī* in the advanced stage of elaboration of *rāga*.

There are two types of compositions, one each for the beginners and the advanced students of music. Serious students of music should always first learn the beginner's compositions in order to easily understand the advanced and difficult compositions later on.

Traditionally speaking, *masit khanī gats* (compositions) are to be played with the following b*ols* (strokes):

dir *da* *dir* *da* *ra* *da* *da* *ra*

Razā khanī gats (compositions) are to be played with the following *bols* (strokes):

da *dir* *dir* *dir* *daऽ* *r, da* *ऽ r,* *da* (8 beats)

Any player, not following these *bols* strictly and traditionally, may not specify the compositions and name them as mentioned here. However, in the modern times, there is a tendency to create something beyond tradition and as such many musicians play *gats* in *tāls* which were never played by any traditional musicians before, and prefer to name them on the *tāls* (cycle) only, e.g. *gat* in the *tāls rūpak, jhaptāl* or in "eleven beats" *tāl*, etc.

Both these styles (*masit khanī* and *razā khanī*) are based on set compositions in *tīntāl* only (a cycle of 16 beats).

The term *pahalī tān* is used by the famous masters (*ustāds*), which does not necessarily mean the *tān* in usage. It is a high-sounding expression, which signifies the character of a *rāga* in its initial stage. Such expression can only be conveyed by the master musicians, having a sound knowledge, based on traditional training.

Any delicacy of any *rāga* can only be explained and justified in *ālāp* and not in *tān*s. The essence of *rāga* can only be felt and explained in the *ālāp* form.

Some Basic Rāgas Based on Ten Thāṭs

RĀGA BILĀWAL

Rāga Bilāwal belongs to *thāṭ* (*mela*) Bilāwal. Its *vādī svara* is *dhaivat* and *samvādī svara* is *gandhār*. *Madhyam svara* is omitted in the ascending order and, therefore, its *jāti* is *ṣaḍava-sampūrṇa*. All the *svara*s used in this *rāga* are *śuddha* (natural). Rāga Bilāwal is played or sung during the first *prahara* of the day.

Ārohī

S, R, G, P, D, N, S

Avarohī

S, N, D, P, M, G, R, S

Initial Phrase (*Pahalī Tān*)

G R G P M G M R, G P D N S

Chalan

MG RG PM GR S

GM RG PM GR SṆ ḌP MG RG

PN Ḍ S

SR GP MG MR, GP ND NS ṘS

ND PM GR GP DN ṠN DP MG

RG PM GR S,

GR GM GR S, GR GP MG RS

ND PM GM, RG PD NR ṠN DP MG RS

RG PD NS ND PM GR GP DN

DP MG RG PM GR SN S

GR GP ND NS ND PM GM RG PM GR S

Note :"R G P M G R S" phrase is taken while concluding the *tān*.

Rāga Bilāwal

Tāl: Tīntāl — *Gat: Masit khanī*

1	2	3	4	5	6	7	8	9	10	11	12	13	14	15	16
+				2				0				3			
					Sthāyī										
											RR	G	PP	N_D	N
											dir	da	dir	da	ra
S	S	S	NS	D	DD	P	D	M	^{G}R	G					
da	da	ra	dir	da	dir	da	ra	da	da	ra					
					Māñjh										
G	PP	D	N	S	RR	G	P	M	^{G}R	G					
da	dir	da	ra	da	dir	da	ra	da	da	ra					
					Antarā										
											RR	G	PP	N_D	N
											dir	da	dir	da	ra
S	S	S	RR	G	PP	MG	R	S	ND	P					
da	da	ra	dir	da	dir	da	ra	da	da	ra					
											GG	P	^{N}DD	N	S
											dir	da	dir	da	ra
D	P	M	GG	R	GG	P	D	M	^{G}R	G					
da	da	ra	dir	da	dir	da	ra	da	da	ra					

Rāga Bilāwal

Tāl: Tīntāl — *Gat: Razā khanī*

1	2	3	4	5	6	7	8	9	10	11	12	13	14	15	16
+				2				0				3			
Elementary Style				***Sthāyī***				M	GG	R	G	P	N	D	N
								da	dir	da	ra	da	ra	da	ra
S	—	D	P	M	G	R	S								
da	ऽ	da	ra	da	ra	da	ra								
				Antarā											
S	—	—	S	N	S	D	N	S	RR	NN	SS	N—	N, D	—D,	P
da	ऽ	ऽ	d	da	ra	da	ra	da	dir	dir	dir	daऽ	r,da	ऽr,	da
S	NN	D	P	M	GG	R	S								
da	dir	da	ra	da	dir	da	ra								

Contd ...

1	2	3	4	5	6	7	8	9	10	11	12	13	14	15	16
+				2				0				3			
Advanced Style				***Sthāyī***											
						GG	MM	G—	G,R	—R,	GG	P	PP	N_D	N
						dir	dir	daऽ	r,da	ऽr,	dir	da	dir	da	ra
S	—	D	P	M	G										
da	ऽ	da	ra	da	ra										
				Antarā											
S	—	—	S	N	S	D	N	S	RR	NN	SS	N—	N,D	—D,	P
—da	ऽ	ऽ	da	da	ra	da	ra	da	dir	dir	dir	daऽ	r,da	ऽr,	da
S	—	D	P	M	G										
da	ऽ	da	ra	da	ra										

RĀGA BHAIRAV

Rāga Bhairav originates from *thāṭ* (*mela*) Bhairav. Its *vādī svara* is *komal dhaivat* (flat sixth) and *samvādī svara* is *komal ṛṣabh* (flat second). *ṛṣabh* and *pañcham* are omitted in the ascending order, therefore, its *jāti* is *auḍava-sampūrṇa*. *Komal ṛṣabh* and *komal dhaivat* are used in this *rāga*. Most suitable time for playing or singing this *rāga* is in the morning.

Ārohī

N, S G, M, D, N, S, R

Avarohī

S, N, D, P, M G, R, S

Initial Pharse (*Pahalī Tān*)

N N G

N S G M, D D P, M, G M R S

Chalan

N G

NS GM DP, MG RS

N N G

NS GM PM, GM DN SN DP MG RS

G

MG RS NS GM PM GM DN SN DP MG RS

N G

GM DN SR SN DP MG MD PM MG RS

N

PM GM RS NS GM P, GM DN

G

SN DP MG RS

Note: In this *rāga* R and D are used with the help of corresponding notes, e.g. G and N,
R D

Rāga Bhairav

Tāl: tīntal *Gat: Masit khanī*

1	2	3	4	5	6	7	8	9	10	11	12	13	14	15	16
+				2				0				3			
					Sthāyī										
											SN	S	GM	P	P
											dir	da	dir	da	ra
N	N								G						
D	D	P	DP	M	PM	G	RGMP	MGM	R	S					
da	da	ra	dir	da	dir	da	ra	da	da	ra					
					Māñjh										
		N							G						
G	MM	D	N	S	GG	MD	P	MGM	R	S					
da	dir	da	ra	da	dir	da	ra	da—	da	ra					
					Antarā										
											GG	M	DD	N	N
											dir	da	dir	da	ra
S	S	S	NS	D	NN	S	R	GM	R	S					
da	da	ra	dir	da	dir	da	ra	da	da	ra					
											R,GM	R	SS	N	S
											dir—	da	dir	da	ra
	N														
S	D	P	MG	M	DD	N	S	MGM	R	S					
da	da	ra	dir	da	dir	da	ra	da—	da	ra					

Rāga Bhairav

Tāl: tīntāl

Gat: Razā khanī

1	2	3	4	5	6	7	8	9	10	11	12	13	14	15	16
+				2				0				3			
Elementary Style				***Sthāyī***											
								S	MM	G	M	—	P	M	P
								da	dir	da	ra	ऽ	da	ra	da
N															
D	—	P	M	G	R	S	N								
da	ऽ	da	ra	da	ra	da	ra								
				Antarā											
D	—	—	M	D	M	D	N	D	N N	S S	R R	S—	S, N	—N,	S
da	ऽ	ऽ	da	da	ra	da	ra	da	dir	dir	dir	daऽ	r,da	ऽr,	da
S	GG	R	M	G	R	S	N	S	R R	N N	S S	N—	N, D	—D,	P
da	dir	da	ra	da	ra	da	ra	da	dir	dir	dir	daऽ	r,da	ऽr,	da
M	D D	P	M	G	R	S	N								
da	dir	da	ra	da	ra	da	ra								

Contd...

1	2	3	4	5	6	7	8	9	10	11	12	13	14	15	16
+				**2**				0				3			
		Advanced Style			***Sthāyī***										
						D D	P P	G—	M, R	—R,	SS	N	S S	G	M
						dir	dir	daऽ	r, da	ऽr,	dir	da	dir	da	ra
ᴺD	—	P	G	—	M										
da	ऽ	da	da	ऽ	ra										
					Antarā										
D	—	—	G	—	M	D	N	D	N N	S S	R R	S—	S, N	—N	S
da	ऽ	ऽ	da	ऽ	da	rऽ	da	da	dir	dir	dir	daऽ	r, da	ऽr,	da
M	D D	P	M	G	M										
da	dir	da	ra	da	ra										

RĀGA TOḌĪ

Rāga Toḍī comes under *thāṭ (mela)* Toḍī. Its *vādī svara* is *komal dhaivat* (Dha) and *samvādī-svara* is *komal gandhār* (Ga). *Pañcham svara* is avoided in the ascending order, thus the *jāti* is *ṣaḍava sampūrṇa*. Along with *tīvra madhyam* (sharp *Ma*), *komal r̥ṣabh* (Re), *komal gandhār* (Ga) and *komal dhaivat* (Da) are used in this *rāga*. Toḍī is sung or played during the second *prahara* of the day.

Ārohī

N, R, G, M, D, N, S, R

Avarohī

S N D P M G R S

Initial Phrase (*Pahalī Tān*)

D N S R G, R G R S.

Chalan

NR GM DM GRS, NR GM ND PM GR S.

GR SN SR GR, GM RG MD ND PM GRS.

DN SR GR, NR GM ND PM GRS

PM GR GM DN SN DP MG RG MD MG RG RS.

DP MG, RG MD, ND PM GR GM, DN SN

DP MG, RG MD MG RG MR GRS.

GR GM, RG RS, NS DN SR, GR GM RG

MD NS RG, DG GR SN DP, MG, RG MD,

SN DP MG RS

Rāga Toḍī

Tāl: tīntāl *Gat: Masit khanī*

1	2	3	4	5	6	7	8	9	10	11	12	13	14	15	16
+				2				0				3			
				Sthāyī							SS	RG	RS	D	N
											dir	da	dir	da	ra
S	S	S	SS	D	DD	P	M	G RG	R	S					
da	da	ra	dir	da	dir	da	ra	da	da	ra					
				Māñjh											
M	DD	N	S	R	GG	DMD	M	GRG	R	S					
da	dir	da	ra	da	dir	da	ra	da	da	ra					
				Antarā							MM	R	GG	M	D
											dir	da	dir	da	ra
S	S	S	NS	D	NN	S	R	G	R	S					
da	da	ra	dir	da	dir	da	ra	da	da	ra					
											RG	R	SS	N	S
											dir	da	dir	da	ra
N	D	P	PP	M	RR	G	MD	GRG	R	S					
da	da	ra	dir	da	dir	da	ra	da	da	ra					

Rāga Toḍī

Tāl: tīntāl *Gat: Razā khanī*

1	2	3	4	5	6	7	8	9	10	11	12	13	14	15	16
+				2				0				3			
Elementary Style				***Sthāyī***				S	RR	G	R	G	R	S	N
								da	dir	da	ra	da	ra	da	ra
S	—	S	N	S	R	G	—								
da	ऽ	da	ra	da	ra	da	ऽ								
								R	GG	R,	G	MM	G,	M	D
				Antarā				da	dir	da,	da	dir	da,	da	ra
S	—	S	S	N	R	S	—								
da	ऽ	da	ra	da	ra	da	ऽ								
								D	GG	R	S	—	N	D	P
								da	dir	da	ra	ऽ	da	ra	da
SN	DM	DN	SR	SN	DP	MG	RS								
dara	dara	dara	dara	dara	dara	dara	dara								

Contd...

Advanced Style				***Sthāyī***											
						RR	GG	R—	R,S	—S,	RR	N	RR	G	M
						dir	dir	daऽ	r,da	ऽr,	dir	da	dir	da	ra
D	—	N	D	M	G										
da	ऽ	da	ra	da	ra										
				Antarā											
D	—	—	M	—	D	N	S	R	GG	RR	SS	N—	N,D	—D,	P
da	ऽ	ऽ	da	ऽ	da	ra	da	da	dir	dir	dir	daऽ	r,da	ऽr,	da
R	GG	M	D	S	—										
da	dir	da	ra	da	ऽ										

RĀGA BHAIRVĪ

Rāga Bhairvī belongs to *thāṭ (mela)* Bhairvī. Its *vādī svara* is *madhyam* (*Ma*) and *samvādī svara* is *ṣaḍaj* (*Sa*). Nothing is avoided in *āroha* and *āvaroha*, therefore, the *jāti* is *sampūrṇa-sampūrṇa*. *r̥ṣabh, gandhār, dhaivat* and *niṣād* used in this *rāga* are *komal* (flat). Rāga Bhairvī is played or sung during the morning hours.

Ārohī

S R G M P D N S (Ascending)

Avarohī

S N D P M G R S (Descending)

Initial Phrase (*Pahalī Tān*)

N S GM PDP, GM $\overset{\text{G}}{\text{R}}$, S

Chalan

NS GM PD PM GM GR S.

DP MP, GM GR SR, NS GM P.

GM DN SR SN DP MG RS.

PM GM GR SR, NS GM PG —M,

DN S, D —N SR GR SN DP MG RS.

DN SR GR G— GM $\overset{\text{G}}{\text{R}}$S. (in slow tempo)

Note: In this composition both the forms of *r̥ṣabh*s are being used and sometimes both *dhaivat*s are also used. In fact, the present Bhairvī is being played or sung with both the *r̥ṣabh*s and *dhaivat*s in Ṭhumrī style. But traditionally speaking, while presenting the Rāga Bhairvī in its purest form all the *komal svara*s (notes) are used. Some scholars also prefer to call it Śuddha Bhairvī.

Rāga Bhairvī

Tāl: Tīntāl | *Gat: Masit khanī*

1	2	3	4	5	6	7	8	9	10	11	12	13	14	15	16
+				2				0				3			
					Sthāyī										
											SR	N	SS	G	M
											dir	da	dir	da	ra
P	D	P	GR	G	PP	D	P	MGM		GR	S				
da	da	ra	dir	da	dir	da	ra	da		da	ra				
					Māñjh										
P	DD	N	S	G	RR	G	M	G R	G R	Sa					
da	dir	da	ra	da	dir	da	ra	da	da	ra					

Contd...

+				2				0				3			
1	2	3	4	5	6	7	8	9	10	11	12	13	14	15	16
					Antarā						D P	G	M M	D	N
											dir	da	dir	da	ra
S	R	S	N N	N	N N	S	S	R S	(N) D	P					
da	da	ra	dir	da	dir	da	ra	da	da	ra					
											N N	R	R R	G	G
											dir	da	dir	da	ra
MGM	(G) R	S	R S	N	S S	D	P	MGM	(G) R	S					
da	da	ra	dir	da	dir	da	ra	da	da	ra					

Rāga Bhairvī

Tāl: Tīntāl | *Gat: Razā khanī*

1	2	3	4	5	6	7	8	9	10	11	12	13	14	15	16
+				2				0				3			
Elementary Style				***Sthāyī***											
												N	S S	G	M
												da	dir	da	ra
P	—	D	P	G	R	G G	M M	R —	R S	— S,	R R				
da	ς	da	ra	da	ra	dir	dir	daς	r,da	ςr,	dir				
				Antarā											
P	—	—	G	—	M	D	N	S	R R	S S	N N	D —	D, P	— M,	P
da	ς	ς	da	ς	da	ra	da	da	dir	dir	dir	daς	r,da	ςr,	da
G	M M	D	N	S	—	N	D	P	M M	G	R				
da	dir	da	ra	da	ς	da	ra	da	dir	da	ra				

Contd...

+				2				0				3			
1	2	3	4	5	6	7	8	9	10	11	12	13	14	15	16
Advanced Style						***Sthāyī***									
						G G	M M	R —	R S	— S,	R R	N	S S	G	M
						dir	dir	daऽ	r, da	ऽr,	da	da	dir	da	ra
P	—	D	P	G	R										
da	ऽ	da	ra	da	ra										
						Antarā									
P	—	—	D	P	D	M	P	D	N N	P P	D D	P —	P, G	— G,	M
da	ऽ	ऽ	da	da	ra	da	ra	da	dir	dir	dir	daऽ	r,da	ऽr,	da
G	MM	D	N	S	—										
da	dir	da	ra	da	ऽ										

RĀGA JAUNPURĪ

Rāga Jaunpurī belongs to *thāṭ* (*mela*) Āsāvarī. Its *vādī svara* is *dhaivat* and *samvādī svara* is *gandhār*. Since *gandhār* and *dhaivat* are avoided in the ascending order, its *jāti* is *auḍava–sampūrṇa*. In this *rāga*, *gandhār*, *dhaivat* and *niṣād* are *komal*. This is sung or played during the second *prahara* of the day.

Ārohī

S R M P N S R G (Ascending)

Avarohī

R S N D P M G R S (Descending)

Initial Phrase (*Pahalī Tān*)

N

R M PS D, P M P G R M P

Chalan

SR MP ND PM GR S.

PM GR SR MP DP MP ND PM GR S.

SR MP DP MP NS, PN SR GR SN

DP MG RS

ND PM GR, SR MP ND PM GR S.

SR MP DP, MP DN SN, PN SR

GR SN DP MG RS.

Note: As there is not much of difference between Rāga Āsāvarī (with *śuddha* R) and Jaunpurī, I am giving only Jaunpurī in order to avoid confusion. Although *dhaivat* is usually taken in *ārohī* but the same is not followed here.

Rāga Jaunpurī

Tāl: Tīntāl *Gat: Masit khanī*

1	2	3	4	5	6	7	8	9	10	11	12	13	14	15	16
+				2				0				3			
					Sthāyī						SS	R	MM	P	S
											dir	da	dir	da	ra
D	D	P	PP	D	MM	PD	MP	MG	R	S					
da	da	ra	dir	da	dir	da	ra	da	da	ra					
					Māñjh										
								M							
M	PP	D	P	S	RR	M	P	G	R	S					
da	dir	da	ra	da	dir	da	ra	da	da	ra					

Contd...

1	2	3	4	5	6	7	8	9	10	11	12	13	14	15	16
+				2				0				3			
									Antarā						
											MM	M	PP	D	P
											dir	da	dir	da	ra
S	S	S	SS	N	SS	R	N	S	D	P					
da	da	ra	dir	da	dir	da	ra	da	da	ra					
											RM	G	RR	S	S
											dir	da	dir	da	ra
NS	ND	P	PP	D	MM	PD	MP	G	R	S					
da	da	ra	dir	da	dir	da	ra	da	da	ra					

Rāga Jaunpurī

Tāl: Tīntāl | *Gat: Razā khanī*

1	2	3	4	5	6	7	8	9	10	11	12	13	14	15	16
+				2				0				3			
Elementary Style				*Sthāyī*				G —	G,R	—R,	S S	R	M M	P	
								daS	r,da	Sr,	dir	da	dir	da	ra
N															
D	—	—	P	M	P	G	R								
da	S	r	da	da	ra	da	ra								
				Antarā											
D	—	—	P	M	P	N	S	R	G G	R R	S S	N —	S,D	—D,	P
da	S	r	da	da	ra	da	ra	da	dir	dir	dir	daS	r,da	Sr,	da
M P	N S	R M	G R	S N	D P	M G	R S								
dara	dara	dara	dara	dara	dara	dara	dara								

Contd...

1	2	3	4	5	6	7	8	9	10	11	12	13	14	15	16
+				2				0				3			
Advanced Style				***Sthāyī***											
								G—	G, R	—R,	S S	R	MM	P	S
								daऽ	r,da	ऽr,	dir	da	dir	da	ra
N D	—	—	P	M	P	G	R								
da	ऽ	r	da	da	ra	da	ra								
								P	—	G	G	R	R	S	—
								da	ऽ	da	ra	da	ra	da	S
N	N	S S	R R	D—	D, P	—M,	P	—							
da	ra	dir	dir	daऽ	r,da	ऽr,	da	r							
				Antarā					M	P P	P	D	—	P	D
									da	dir	da	da	r	da	ra
S	—	S	S	N	N	S	—	—	P	N	S	R	G	R	S
da	r	da	ra	da	ra	da	r	ऽ	da	ra	da	da	ra	da	ra
N	S N	R S	N S	D—	D, P	—M,	P	P	G G	R	G	S	R	N	S
da	dara	dara	dara	daऽ	r,da	ऽr,	da	da	dir	da	ra	da	ra	da	ra
M	P P	N N	D D	G—	G, R	—R,	S								
da	dir	dir	dir	daऽ	r, da	ऽr,	da								

RĀGA YAMAN

Rāga Yaman is originated from *thāṭ* (*mela*) Yaman. Its *vādī svara* is *gandhār* and *samvādī svara* is *niṣād*. All the notes are used in the ascending and the descending orders, therefore, its *jāti* is *sampūrṇa-sampūrṇa*. It is sung or played during the *pratham prahara* (1st part) of the night. *Tīvra* (sharp) *madhyam* (fourth note) is used in this *rāga*. Rest of the notes are all *śuddha* (natural).

Ārohī

N, R, G, M, P, D, N, R (Ascending)

Avarohī

S, N, D, P M, G, R, S, (Descending)

Initial Phrase (*Pahali Tān*)

N R G R G, G R, N R S

Chalan

NR GM PM GR S.

NR GM ND PM GR S.

PM GR, ND PM GR GM PD PM GR S.

NR GR GM, RG MD, NR GR SN DP.

MG, RG MN DP MG RG RS.

PM GR, ND PM GR, GR SN DP MG

MD NR SN DP MG RG MP MG RS.

GR MG PM DP ND PM GR SN SR

GR SN DP MD NR GR GM PM GR S.

Note: Although in *ārohī* all the notes ate taken, but to give a colourful picture to the *rāga*, it is often taken as "N R G" instead of "S R G" which is allowed.

Rāga Yaman

Tāl: Tīntāl *Gat: Masit khanī*

1	2	3	4	5	6	7	8	9	10	11	12	13	14	15	16
+				2				0				3			
				Sthāyī											
											NN	R	GG	M	P
											dir	da	dir	da	ra
P N	D	P	PP	M	RR	G	M P	RG	R	S					
da	da	ra	dir	da	dir	da	ra	da	da	ra					
				Māñjh											
M	DD	N	R	G	RR	G	MP	RG	R	S					
da	dir	da	ra	da	dir	da	ra	da	da	ra					

Contd...

1	2	3	4	5	6	7	8	9	10	11	12	13	14	15	16
+				2				0				3			
					Antarā										
											PP	^{M}G	MM	^{N}D	N
											dir	da	dir	da	ra
S	S	S	SS	N	DD	N	R	G	R	S					
da	da	ra	dir	da	dir	da	ra	da	da	ra					
											GG	R	SS	N	S
											dir	da	dir	da	ra
N	D	P	PP	M	RR	G	MP	RG	R	S					
da	da	ra	dir	da	dir	da	ra	da	da	ra					

Rāga Yaman

Tāl: Tīntāl *Gat: Raza Khani*

1	2	3	4	5	6	7	8	9	10	11	12	13	14	15	16
+				2				0				3			
Elementary Style				**Sthāyī**											
								N	R R	N N	G G	R —	R, N	— N,	R
								da	dir	dir	dir	daऽ	r,da	ऽr	da
G	—	—	P P	R	G G	R	S								
da	ऽ	ऽ	dir	da	dir	da	ra								
				Antarā											
G	—	—	R	G	M M	P	D	M	N N	D D	P P	M —	M, R	— R,	G
da	ऽ	ऽ	da	da	dir	da	ra	da	dir	dir	dir	da ऽ	r,da	ऽr,	da
M	N N	D	P	R	G	R	S								
da	dir	da	ra	da	ra	da	ra								

Contd...

+				2				0				3			
1	2	3	4	5	6	7	8	9	10	11	12	13	14	15	16
Advanced Style					**_Sthāyī_**										
						MM	PP	M—	M,G	—G,	RR	G	MM	D	N
						dir	dir	daऽ	r,da	ऽr,	dir	da	dir	da	ra
P	—	—	M	G	R										
da	ऽ	ऽ	da	da	ra										
					Antarā										
P	—	—	M	G	R	G	M	P	MM	RR	GG	R—	R,N	—N,	R
da	ऽ	ऽ	da	da	ra	da	ra	da	dir	dir	dir	daऽ	r,da	ऽr,	da
D	NN	D,	N	—	R	G	R	G	MM	GG	MM	D—	D,M	—M,	D
da	dir	da,	da	ऽ	ra	da	ra	da	dir	dir	dir	daऽ	r,da	ऽr,	da
MP	DN	SN	DP	MG	RS										
dara	dara	dara	dara	dara	dara										

RĀGA MARWĀ

Rāga Marwā belongs to *thāṭ* (*mela*) Marwā. Its *vādī svara* is *ṛṣabh* and *samvādī svara* is *dhaivat. Pañcham svara* is avoided both in the ascending and the descending orders; therefore, the *jāti* is *ṣaḍava-ṣaḍava. Komal ṛṣabh* (flat), *tīvra madhyam* (sharp) along with rest of the *śuddha* (natural) *svara*s are used in this *rāga*. This *rāga* is sung or played during the last *prahara* of the day.

Ārohī

N R G M D N S (Ascending)

Avarohī

R N D M G R S. (Descending)

Initial Phrase (*Pahalī Tān*)

D N R, R N D, D S

Chalan

NR GM DM D, DM GR, ND NR
DR S.
RG MD DM GR ND MD NR GR
DM GR, GM D, DM GR ND S.
MD NR, ND, MD MG R—, RG MD,
DM GR, ND S.

Rāga Marwā

Tāl: Tīntāl *Gat: Masit khanī*

1	2	3	4	5	6	7	8	9	10	11	12	13	14	15	16
+				2				0				3			
					Sthāyī										
											R̲R̲	G	M̍M̍	D	M̍
											dir	da	dir	da	ra
D	D	D	DD	M̍	GG	R̲	D	M̍	G	R̲					
da	da	da	dir	da	dir	da	ra	da	da	ra					
					Māñjh										
M̍	DD	N	R̲	G	R̲R̲	D	M̍	G	R̲	S					
da	dir	da	ra	da	dir	da	ra	da	da	ra					

Contd...

1	2	3	4	5	6	7	8	9	10	11	12	13	14	15	16
+				2				0				3			
					Antarā						DD	R̲	GG	M̍	D
											dir	da	dir	da	ra
R̲	R̲	S	SS	N	DD	N	R̲	G	R̲	S					
da	da	ra	dir	da	dir	da	ra	da	da	ra					
											NN	R̲	GR̲	N	D
											dir	da	dir	da	ra
M̍	D	D	R̲R̲	G	M̍M̍	D	M̍	G	R̲	S					
da	da	ra	dir	da	dir	da	ra	da	da	ra					

Rāga Marwā

Tāl: Tīntāl *Gat: Razā khanī*

1	2	3	4	5	6	7	8	9	10	11	12	13	14	15	16
+				2				0				3			
Elementry Style					*Sthāyī*										
												N	R R	G	M
												da	dir	da	ra
D	—	D	—	M	G	R R	D D	M—	M, G	— G	R				
da	ऽ	da	ऽ	da	ra	dir	dir	daऽ	r,da	ऽr,	da				
					Antarā										
D	—	—	M	—	D	N	R	R	N N	D D	M M	G—	G, R	—R,	D
da	ऽ	ऽ	da	ऽ	da	ra	da	da	dir	dir	dir	daऽ	r,da	ऽr,	da
M	D D	M,	G	—	R,	D	M	D	M M	G	R				
da	dir	da,	da	ऽ	ra,	da	ra	da	dir	da	ra				

Contd...

+				2				0				3			
1	2	3	4	5	6	7	8	9	10	11	12	13	14	15	16
Advanced Style				***Sthāyī***											
		S	NN	S,	D	—	D,	M	DD	M	G	R,	R	—	N
		da	dir	da,	da	ꜱ	ra,	da	dir	da	ra	da,	daꜱ	r,da	ꜱr,
D	—														
da	ꜱ														
				Antarā											
D	—	—	N	—	R	G	M	D	NN	RR	GG	N—	—R	—N,	D—
da	ꜱ	ꜱ	da	ꜱ	ra	da	ra	da	dir	dir	dir	daꜱ	ꜱr	da,	daꜱ
—N	D,	M—	—D	M,	G—	—M	G,	R	G	R,	N	RR	G	M	D
ꜱr	da,	daꜱ	ꜱr	da,	daꜱ	ꜱr	da,	da	ra	da,	da	dir	da	ra	da
—	—														
S	S														

RĀGA PŪRVĪ

Rāga Pūrvī belongs to *thāṭ* (*mela*) Pūrvī. Its *vādī svara* is *gandhār* and *samvādī svara* is *niṣād*. Since nothing is avoided in the ascending and the descending orders, the *jāti* falls under the category of *sampūrṇa-sampūrṇa*. Along with both the types of *madhyam-śuddha* and *tīvra* (natural and sharp), *komal ṛṣabh* (flat) and *komal dhaivat* (flat) are used in this *rāga*. Rāga Pūrvī is to be performed in the evening.

Ārohī

N R G M D N S R (Ascending)

Avarohī

S N D P M G M G R S (Descending)

Initial Phrase (*Pahali Tān*)

N R G M P M, G M G R G

Chalan

NR GM PM, GM GR GR S

PM GM GR G, NN DP MP GM GR

G, MG RS

NR GM PM, GM DN SN DP MP, GM

GR G, RG MD MG, MG RG RS.

PM GM DN SN DP, GM GR G, MD ND

PM GM GR, RG MP MG, MG RG RS

Note: *Śuddha madhyam* (natural) is always taken along with *śuddha gandhār*.

Rāga Pūrvī

Tāl: Tīntāl *Gat: masit khanī*

1	2	3	4	5	6	7	8	9	10	11	12	13	14	15	16
+				2				0				3			
					Sthāyī										
											NN	R	GG	M	D
											dir	da	dir	da	ra
P	P	P	PP	M	GM	G	R	MG	R	S					
da	da	ra	dir	da	dir	da	ra	da	da	ra					
					Māñjh										
M	PP	D	N	R	GG	M	P	GM	GR	G					
da	dir	da	ra	da	dir	da	ra	da	da	ra					

Contd...

1	2	3	4	5	6	7	8	9	10	11	12	13	14	15	16
+				2				0				3			
					Antarā						PP	MG	MM	D	N
											dir	da	dir	da	ra
S	S	S	NN	R	GG	R	S	N	D	P					
da	da	ra	dir	da	dir	da	ra	da	da	ra					
											RG	R	SS	N	D
											dir	da	dir	da	ra
PM	GM	G	RR	G	MM	P	M	RG	R	S					
da	da	ra	dir	da	dir	da	ra	da	da	ra					

Rāga Pūrvī

Tāl: Tīntāl *Gat: Razā khanī*

1	2	3	4	5	6	7	8	9	10	11	12	13	14	15	16
+				2				0				3			
Elementary Style				***Sthāyī***											
								R	G G	R,	G	—	P,	M	D
								da	dir	da,	da	ऽ	ra,	da	ra
P	—	P	M	G	R	S	N								
da	ऽ	da	ra	da	ra	da	ra								
				Antarā											
P	—	P	M	G	M	G,	—	—	N N	D D	N N	D—	D, P	— P,	D
da	ऽ	da	ra	da	ra	da,	ऽ	ऽ	dir	dir	dir	daऽ	r,da	ऽr,	da
M	PM	G	M	G	R	S	N								
da	dir	da	ra	da	ra	da	ra								

Contd...

Advanced Style				Sthāyī											
						PP	DD	M	P	—	G	—	M,	G	R
						dir	dir	da	da	r	da	ऽ	ra,	da	ra
G	—	—	R	—	S										
da	ऽ	ऽ	da	ऽ	ra										
				Antarā											
G	—	—	R	—	S,	N	R	G	MM	DD	NN	S—	S,R	—R,	S
da	ऽ	ऽ	da	ऽ	ra,	da	ra	da	dir	dir	dir	daऽ	r,da	ऽr,	da
N	SS	N,	D	—	P										
da	dir	da,	da	ऽ	ra										

RĀGA KHAMĀJ

Rāga Khamāj comes under *thāṭ* (*mela*) Khamāj. Its *vādī svara* is *gandhār* and *samvādī svara* is *niṣād*. Both the forms of *niṣād* — *śuddha* and *komal* (natural and flat) — are used in this *rāga*. All the other *svaras* used are *śuddha*. In the ascending order *r̥ṣabh* is omitted, therefore, its *jāti* is *ṣaḍava-sampūrna*. *Komal niṣād* is used only in the descending order. Rāga Khamāj is played or sung during the second *prahara* of the night.

Ārohī

N, S, G, M, P, D, N, S (Ascending)

Avarohī

S, N, D, P, M, G, R, S, (Desceding)

Initial Phrase (*Pahalī Tān*)

G M P D N S N S, D N D N, P D S S, N D G M G.

Chalan

GM PD NS NS PN ND N, DNS NS ND PD P, GM PD ND PM GM G.

GM PD NS ND PM GM G.

NS GM PD ND PD NS NS, DN PD ND GM G.

GM PD ND PM GM GR NS.

Rāga Khamāj

Tāl: Tīntāl *Gat: Masit khanī*

1	2	3	4	5	6	7	8	9	10	11	12	13	14	15	16
+				2				0				3			
					Sthāyī						SN	S	GM	P	D
											dir	da	dir	da	ra
N	N	S	SS	N̲	DD	P	P	G	M	G					
da	da	ra	dir	da	dir	da	ra	da	da	ra					
					Māñjh										
N	SS	G	M	P	DD	N	S	N̲D	GM	G					
da	dir	da	ra	da	dir	da	ra	da	da	ra					

Contd...

+				2				0				3			
1	2	3	4	5	6	7	8	9	10	11	12	13	14	15	16
					Antarā						MG	M	ND	P	D
											dir	da	dir	da	ra
N	N	S	NN	N	NN	S	S	S	N	D					
da	da	ra	dir	da	dir	da	ra	da	da	ra					
											GM	G	SS	N	S
											dir	da	dir	da	ra
S	N	D	MG	M	ND	P	D	G	M	G					
da	da	ra	dir	da	dir	da	ra	da	da	ra					

Rāga Khamāj

Tāl: Tīntāl *Gat: Razā khanī*

1	2	3	4	5	6	7	8	9	10	11	12	13	14	15	16
+				2				0				3			
Elementary Style				***Sthāyī***								G	M M	P	D
												da	dir	da	ra
N	—	S	—	P	D	S N	R S	N —	N, D	— D,	P				
da	ऽ	da	ऽ	da	ra	dara	dara	daऽ	r,da	ऽ r,	da				
				Antarā								G	M M	N	D
												da	dir	da	ra
G	M	G	—	S	N N	S	G	—	M	P	D				
da	ra	da	ऽ	da	dir	da	da	ऽ	ra	da	ra				
												N	S	S N	R S
												da	ra	dara	dara
N —	N, D	— P	D	P	D D	N,	S	—	N	D	P				
daऽ	r,da	ऽr,	da	da	dir	da,	da	ऽ	ra	da	ra				

Contd...

1	2	3	4	5	6	7	8	9	10	11	12	13	14	15	16
+				2				0				3			
Advanced Style				***Sthāyī***											
				P	D	SN	RS	N—	N, D	—P,	D	G	GM	P	D
				da	ra	dara	dara	daऽ	r,da	ऽr,	da	da	dir	da	ra
N	—	S	—												
da	r	da	ऽ												
				Antarā											
N	—	S,	D	—	N	P	D	N	SS	RR	SS	N—	N, D	—D,	P
da	ऽ	ra,	da	ऽ	ra,	da	ra	da	dir	dir	dir	daऽ	r, da	ऽr,	da
G	MM	N	D	P	G	M	G	S	NN	S,	G	—	M,	P	D
da	dir	da	ra	da	ra	da	ra	da	dir	da,	da	ऽ	ra,	da	ra
N	—	S	—												
da	r	da	ऽ												

RĀGA KĀFĪ

Rāga Kāfī belongs to *thāṭ* (*mela*) Kāfi. Its *vādi svara* is *pañcham* and *samvādi svara* is *ṣaḍaj*. All the notes are used in the ascending as well as the descending order, therefore, its *jāti* is *sampūrṇa-sampūrṇa*. *Gandhār* and *niṣad svaras* used in this *rāga* are *komal* (flat). Rāga Kāfī is to be performed in the middle of the night.

Ārohī

S, R, G M, P, D, N, S (Ascending)

Avarohī

S, N, D, P, M, G, R, S (Descending)

Initial Phrase (*Pahali Tān*)

R R G, R G M P D N D, N D P.

Chalan

SR GM P, DP MP GR, SN SS RR GG

MM P.

PM PD NS ND PM MM PG —R, RN

DN PD MP RG RM GR SN S.

PM GR GM PD ND PM GR SN S.

Rāga Kāfī

Tāl: Tīntāl | *Gat: Masit khanī*

1	2	3	4	5	6	7	8	9	10	11	12	13	14	15	16
+				2				0				3			
					Sthāyī						RP	G	RR	G	M
											dir	da	dir	da	ra
P	P	P	MM	D	DD	N	D	MP	G	R					
da	da	ra	dir	da	dir	da	ra	da	da	ra					
					Māñjh										
P	DD	N	S	R	GG	M	P	MP	G	R					
da	dir	da	ra	da	dir	da	ra	da	da	ra					

Contd...

				Antarā											
											N D	M	P P	D	N
											dir	da	dir	da	ra
S	S	S	D N	R	R R	G	R	S R	N	D					
da	da	ra	dir	da	dir	da	ra	da	da	ra					
											R M	G	R R	S	R
											dir	da	dir	da	ra
N	D	P	M M	M	P P	D M	P D	M P	M G	R					
da	da	ra	dir	da	dir	da	ra	da	da	ra					

Rāga Kāfī

Tāl: Tīntāl *Gat : Razā khanī*

1	2	3	4	5	6	7	8	9	10	11	12	13	14	15	16
+				2				0				3			
Elementry Style					*Sthāyī*			S	R R	R,	G	—,	M	P	M
								da	dir	da,	da	r,	da	ra	da
P	—	P	M	G	R	S	N								
da	r	da	ra	da	ra	da	ra								
					Antarā										
P	—	—	M	P	D	N	S	N	D D	M M	P P	M —	M, G	— G,	R
da	ऽ	r	da	da	ra	da	ra	da	dir	dir	dir	daऽ	r,da	ऽr,	da
R	N N	D	N	P	D D	M	P	G	M M	P P	M M	G —	G, R	— S,	R
da	dir	da	ra	da	dir	da	ra	da	dir	dir	dir	daऽ	r,da	ऽr,	da
P	—	P	M	G	R	S	N								
da	r	da	ra	da	ra	da	ra								

Contd...

1	2	3	4	5	6	7	8	9	10	11	12	13	14	15	16
+				2				0				3			
Advanced Style						***Sthāyī***									
						DD	PP	M—	P,G	—G,	R	R	GG	M	M
						dir	dir	daऽ	r,da	ऽr,	da	da	dir	da	ra
P	—	P	M	G	R										
da	r	da	ra	da	ra										
						Antarā									
P	—	P	M	P	D	N	S	N	DD	MM	PP	G—	G,R	—S,	R
da	r	da	ra	da	ra	da	ra	da	dir	dir	dir	daऽ	r,da	ऽr,	da
R	GG	M	M	P	—										
da	dir	da	ra	da	ऽ										

8

Rāgas Composed by Pandit Debu Chaudhuri

1. Rāga Biśveśvarī

Svaras used	:	Dha and Ni *komal*, rest of the *svaras* are *śuddha*.
Mela	:	*Charukeśi* (Karnatic *mela*)
Vādī	:	'Pa' (*pañcham*)
Samvādī	:	'Sa' (*ṣaḍja*)
Suitable time	:	Second quarter of the night
Jāti	:	*Auḍava-sampūrṇa*
Note	:	Mālkauṁs-*aṅg*, in ascending (*āroha*) and Kānhaḍā-*aṅg* in descending (*avaroha*) orders.
	:	*Gandhār* (Ga) remaining *śuddha*. Ga Ma Re Sa or Ga Ma Re Ni Sa is used while coming to Sa. This gives an added feeling of Rāga Rāgeśrī in *mandra saptak* Dha Ni and then Sa, Ga, Ma, Re in *madhya saptak* and is to be concluded with Ni Sa, which combines both *aṅgas* of Mālkauṁs and Rāgeśrī. Dha, Ni, Pa, Ma, Ga, Ma, Re Sa, gives a clear pictue of *gandhār*. But Ga being *śuddha*, again gives a new shade and colour.
Āroha	:	Sa Ga Ma Dha Ni Sa.
Avaroha	:	Sa Ni Dha Ni Pa Ma Ga Ma Re Sa.
Pakaṛ	:	Sa Ga Ma Dha Ni Pa, Ni Pa Ma Pa Ga Ma Re Ni, Sa Ga Ma Re Sa.

Chalan : (1) Ga Ma Re Sa, Ni, Sa Dha Ni, Sa Ga Ma Pa Ga Ma Re Sa.

: (2) Sa Ga Ma Pa Ga Ma Re Sa Ni, Sa Dha Ni Sa Ga, Sa Ga Ma Dha Ni Pa, Ma Pa Ga Ma Ga, Sa Ga Ma Pa Ga Ma Re Sa.

: (3) Ni Sa Dha Ni Sa Re, Re Sa Ni Sa Dha Ni, Pa Ma Ga Ma Dha Ni Sa.

: (4) Dha Ni Sa Ga Ma Re-Sa, Ni Sa Dha Ni Pa Ma Ga Ma Re Sa.

: (5) Sa- Dha Ni Sa, Dha Ni Pa Ma Ga Ma Re Sa.

: (6) GaMa Dha Ni Sa, Dha Ni Sa Ga, Ga-Re Ga Ma Ga Re Sa Ni, Ni, Sa-Re Ni Sa Dha Ni, Pa, Ma-Pa Ga- Ma Dha Ni Sa, Re Sa Ni Sa Dha Ni Pa Ma Ga Ma Re Sa.

: (7) Pa Ga Ma Re Sa Ni Sa Dha Ni Sa Ga Ma Dha, Ga Ma Dha Ni Sa Ni Sa Dha Ni Pa Ma Ga Ma Re Sa.

: (8) Sa Ga Ma Pa Ga Ma Re Sa NS Ga Ma Dha, Ga Ma Dha Ni Sa Re Sa Ni Sa Dha Ni Pa Ma Ga Ma Re Sa.

: (9) Ga Ma Re Sa, Dha Ni Pa Ma Ga Ma Re Sa.

2. Rāga Kalyāṇī Bilāwal

Svaras used : Both *madhyams* are used, rest of all *svaras* are *śuddha*.

Vādī : "Ga" (*gandhār*)

Samvādī : "Ni" (*niṣād*)

Suitable time : Morning

Jāti : *Ṣaḍava-sampūrṇa*

Note : This *Rāga* is created by combining two *melas*, viz. Yaman and Bilāwal.

Āroha : Sa Re Ga Pa Dha Ni Sa Re

Avaroha : Sa Ni Dha Pa Ma Pa Ga M̍a Ga Re Ga Re Sa.

Pakaṛ : Ni Re Ga Pa Ma Ga, Ma Ga M̍a Re Pa, Ma Pa Ga Ma Ga, Ga Re Sa Ni, Dha Ni Sa.

Chalan (1) Pa Ma Ga M̍a Ga Re Ga Re Sa Ni, Dha Ni, Re Ga Ma Ga, Ga Re Sa Ni Sa.

(2) Ga M̍a Re Pa Ma M̍a, Ga Ma Re, Ga M̍a Dha Pa M̍a, Ga M̍a Ga Re Ga, Ni Re Ga M̍a Ga, Dha Pa M̍a Pa Ga M̍a Ga Re, Ga Re Sa Ni Sa.

(3) Ga Ma Re Pa, M̍a Pa, M̍a Dha Pa, M̍a Pa, Ga Ma Re Ga M̍a Ga, Ni Re Ga Ma Ga, Dha Pa Ma Pa Ga Ma Ga Re Ga, Re Ga Pa Ma Dha Pa Ma Pa, Ga Ma Ga-Re, Ga Re Sa Ni, Dha Ni Sa.

(4) Ga M̍a Re Pa, Ma Ni Dha Pa, Ma Pa Ma Ga, Pa, Ni Dha Ni Sa, Ma Dha Pa Sa, Ni Re Sa Ni Dha Pa, Ma Dha Ma Ni Dha Pa, Ga Ma Re Ga Ma Dha Pa Ma Pa Ga Ma Ga Re. Sa Ni, Dha Ni Re Ga, Ma Ga, Ga Re Sa.

3. Rāga Āshiqui Lalit

Svaras used : 'Re' *komal*, both *madhyams* are used, rest of the *svaras* are *śuddha*, 'Pa' omited

Mela : Marwā

Vādī : 'Ma' (*madhyam*)

Samvādī : 'Sa' (*ṣaḍja*)

Suitable time : Morning

Jāti : *Ṣaḍava-ṣaḍava*

Note : More emphasis on Marwā *aṅg*.

Āroha : Ni Re Ga M̍a Dha Ni Sa Re.

Avaroha : Sa Ni Dha M̍a Ma Ga Re Sa.

Pakaṛ : Ni-Re Ga Ma, Ma Ma, Ga Re, Ma Ga, Ga Re Ni Dha Re, Sa.

Chalan : (1) Ni Re Ga Ma, Ma Ma, Ga Re, Ni Re Ni Dha, Ma Dha, Ni Re, Ni Dha, Re, Sa.

(2) Dha Ma Ga Re, Ga Ma Ma Ma, Ga Re, Ga Ma Dha Ni, Ma Ni Dha Ma, Ga Re, Ni Re Ni Dha Re, Sa.

(3) Ni Re Ga Ma Ma Ma Ga Re, Ga Ma Dha Ni, Ma Ni Dha Ma, Ga Re, Ni Re, Ga Ma Ma Ma Ga Re, Ga Re Ni Dha Re, Sa.

(4) Ga Re Ni Dha, Ni Re Ga Re Ni Dha Re Sa. Dha-Ma Dha Ma Ma Ga Re Sa, Ni Re Ga Ma Ma Ma.

(5) Ni Re Ni Dha, Ni Re Ga Ma Ma Ma Ga Re, Ma Ga Re Ni Sa.

(6) Re Ga Ma Ma Ga Re, Ma Ma Ga Re, Dha Ma Ga Re, Ni Dha Ma Ga Re, Ni Re Ni Dha Re.

(7) Dha Ma Ga Re Ga Ma, Ma Ma Ga Re, Ga Ma Dha Ma Dha, Ma Dha Ni Re Ni Dha, Ni Re, Ga Ma Ma Ma, Ga Re, Ni Re Ni Dha Ma Dha Ma Ma Ga Re, Ga Ma Ma Ma, Ga Re Ni Dha Re, – Sa.

4. Rāga Palās Sāraṅg

Svaras used : *Niṣād komal*, both *madhyam*s are used, rest of the *svara*s are *śuddha.*

Mela : Kāfī

Vādī : 'Pa' (*pañcham*)

Samvādī : 'Re' (*ṛṣabh*)

Suitable time : Between second and third quarters of the noon.

Jāti : *Auḍava-ṣaḍava*

Note : This *rāga* is created by the amalgamation of *rāga*s 'Bhimpalāsī' and Suddha Sāraṅg.

Āroha : Sa Ra Ma Pa Ni Sa.

Avaroha : Sa Ni Dha Pa Ma Pa, Re Ma Re Sa.

Pakaṛ : Re Ma Pa Ni Dha Pa, Re Ma Re Sa Ni Sa Re Ma Pa.

Chalan : (1) Re Sa Ni Sa, Re Ma Pa Dha Ma Pa, Re Ma Re Sa Ni Sa Re.

(2) Dha Pa Ma Pa, Re Ma Re Sa Ni Sa.

(3) Re Ma Pa Ni Dha Pa Ma Pa, Re Ma Re Sa Ni Sa.

(4) Pa Ni Sa Re Ni Sa Ni Dha Pa Ma, Pa Ni Dha Pa Ma Pa, Re Ma Re Sa.

(5) Sa Ni Dha Pa Ma Pa, Re Ma Pa Ni Dha Ma Re Pa, Ma Pa Ni Sa.

(6) Sa Ni Dha Ma Pa, Re Ma Re Sa Ni Sa Re Ma Pa, Re Ma Pa Ni Sa, Pa Ni Sa Re Ni Sa Ni Dha Pa Ma, Pa Ni Dha Pa Ma Pa, Re Ma Re Sa Ni Sa Re Re Ma Re Sa, Ni Sa Re Ma Pa Ni Sa, Re Sa Ni Sa Ni Dha Pa Dha Ma Pa, Re Ma Re Sa Ni Sa Re.

7) Ni Sa Re Ma Pa Ma, Re Ma Pa Ni Sa Ni, Ma Pa Ni Sa Pa Ni Sa Re Ma Pa Ma Re Ma Re Se Ni Dha Pa Ma Pa Re Ma Pa Ni Sa Re Sa Re.

(8) Re Ma Re Sa Ni Sa ReSa Ni Sa Ni Dha Ma Pa Sa Ni Dha Pa Dha Ma Pa Re Ma Re Sa Ni Sa Re Sa Re.

5. Rāga Anurañjanī

Svaras used : 'Ma', not taken Dha and Ni *komal*, rest of the *svaras* are *śuddha*.

Vādī : 'Pa' (*pañcham*)

Samvādī : 'Sa' (*ṣaḍja*)

Suitable time : Morning

Jāti : *Ṣaḍava-ṣaḍava*

Note : This *rāga* has the base of Bilāwal *mela* in the first part of the *saptak* (*pūrvāṅga*) and *Bhairvī mela* in the second half of the *saptak (uttarāṅga).*

Āroha : Sa Re Ga Pa Dha Ni Sa.

Avaroha : Sa Ni Dha Pa Ga Re Sa.

Pakaṛ : Re Ga Pa Dha Pa, Ga Re, Ni Dha Sa.

Chalan : (1) Sa Re Ga Pa Dha Pa Ga Re, Sa Ni Dha Sa.

(2) Sa Re Ga, Re Re Ga, Sa Sa Re, Ni Sa, Ni Dha Pa, Dha Ni Sa Re Ga Re, Ni Dha Sa.

(3) Sa Re Ga Pa, Dha Pa Ga Re, Re Sa Ni Dha Sa.

(4) Re Ga Pa Dha Pa, Sa Re Ga Pa, Pa Ga, Dha Pa Ga, Ni Dha Pa Ga Re, Ni Dha Sa.

(5) Re Ga Pa Dha Pa, Ni Dha Pa Ga, Ga Pa Dha Ni Dha Pa Ga, Pa Ga Re Ni Dha Sa.

(6) Ga Pa Dha Ni Sa, Ni Dha Sa, Sa Dha Ni Dha Pa, Dha Ni Sa, Re Sa Ni Sa Dha Pa, Pa Ga, Ga Pa Dha Ni, Ni Ni Pa Ga, Ga Re Ni Dha Sa.

(7) Ga Pa Dha Ni Sa, Ni Sa Re Ga, Re Ga Sa Re Ni Sa Ni Dha Pa, Sa Ni Dha Pa Ga, Ga Pa Dha Ni, Ni Dha Pa Ga, Ga Re Ni Dha Sa.

6. Rāga Śivamañjarī

Svaras used : Ga, Dha *komal*, rest of the *svaras* are *śuddha*.

Mela : Kirwānī

Vādī : Pa (*pañcham*)

Samvādī : Sa (*ṣaḍja*)

Suitable time : Evening

Jāti : *Auḍava-sampūrṇa*

Note : In *ārohī*, this *rāga* has the *aṅg* of *Śivrañjanī*

Āroha : Sa Re Ga Pa Dha Sa.

Avaroha : Sa Ni Dha Pa Ma Ga Re Sa.

Pakaṛ : Sa Re Ga Pa, Dha Pa Ma Ga Re, Ni Dha Sa. Pa Dha Sa Re Ga, Ga Re Ni Dha Sa, Dha Pa Ma Ga Re, Re Ga Pa Ma Ga Re, Ni Dha Sa.

Chalan : (1) Sa Re Ga Pa, Dha Pa Ma Ga, Ra, Ma Ga Re Ni Dha Sa.

(2) Sa Re Ga Pa, Dha Ni Dha Pa, Ma Ga Re, Re Ga Ma Ga Re, Sa Ni Dha Sa.

(3) Sa Re Ga Pa Ma Ga, Dha Pa Ma Ga Re Sa Re, Ga Ma Ga Re Sa Ni Dha Sa.

(4) Ga Pa Dha, Sa, Re Sa Ni Dha Ni Dha Pa, Dha Pa Ma Ga Re, Ni Ni Dha Pa Ma Ga Re Re Sa, Re, Sa.

(5) Pa Dha Sa, Ga Re Ni Dha Sa, Pa Dha Sa Re Ga Re Ni Dha Pa, Pa Ma Ga Re Ni Dha Sa, Sa Re Ga Pa Dha Ni Dha Pa Ma Ga Re, Pa Ma Ga Re Sa, Ni Dha Sa.

7. Rāga Svanandeśvarī

Svaras used : Ga and Ni k*omal*, all other *svara*s are *śuddha*

Mela : Kāfī

Vādī : Pa (*pañcham*)

Samvādī : Sa (*ṣaḍja*)

Suitable time : Evening

Jāti : *Auḍava-sampūrṇa*

Note : In this *rāga* there is 'Śivrañjanī' in the *āroha* and 'Kāfī' in the *avaroha*. Sometimes we also find traces of the 'Rāga Nīlāmbarī' while using the following notes: Ga Re Ni Dha Sa Dha Ni Ga Re.

Āroha : Sa Re Ga Pa Dha Sa.

Avaroha : Sa Ni Dha Pa Ma Ga Re Sa.

Pakaṛ : Sa Re-Ga Pa, Pa Dha Ni Dha Pa Ma Ga, Re, Ga Re, Ni Dha Sa.

Chalan : (1) Sa Re Ga Pa, Ga Pa Dha Ni Dha Pa, Ma Dha Pa Dha Ma Ga Re, Re Ga, Pa Ma Ga, Ma Ga Re, Ga Re Sa Re Ni Dha Sa.

(2) Sa Re Ga Pa, Ga Pa Dha Ni Dha Pa Ma Ga, Re Sa Ni Dha Sa, Pa Ma Ga, Ni Dha Sa, Ni Dha Pa Ma Ga, Ma Ga Re, Ga Re, Sa Ni Dha Sa.

(3) Dha Sa Re Ga, Ga Pa Ma Ga, Re Ga Re, Sa, Sa Ni Dha Sa.

(4) Ga Pa Dha Sa Ni Dha Sa. Pa Dha Sa Re Ga, Ga Re Ni Dha Sa.

(5) Sa Re Ni Dha Ma Pa Dha, Ma_{Ga} Re, Ga Pa Dha Ni Dha Pa Dha Sa, Ni Dha Pa Ma Ga Re Sa.

(6) Ni Dha Pa Dha Sa.

(7) Sa Ni Dha Pa Dha Pa, Ga Pa Dha Ni Dha Pa Ma Ga, Pa Ma Ga-Re, Ma Ga Re, Ni Dha Sa.

8. Rāga Prabhātī Mañjarī

*Svara*s used : Re, Ga and Ni *komal* and all other *svara*s are *śuddha*.

Note : This *rāga* is composed of the *mela* Bhairvī Kāfī. This *rāga* is dedicated in memory of my wife Manjusree, Use of Re Ga Re Sa gives a colour and shade to Toḍī *aṅg*.

Vādī : Ma (*madhyam*)

Samvādī : Sa (*ṣaḍja*)

Suitable time : Morning

Jāti *Ṣaḍava-sampūrṇa.*

Mela : Nāṭaka Priyā

Note : This *rāga* cannot be placed in any north Indian *mela paddhati* of Bhatkhande but it can be placed in the 10th *mela* Rāga Nāṭaka Priyā *of* Karnatic *mela*.

Āroha : Sa Re Ma Pa Dha Ni-Sa

Avaroha : Sa Ni Dha-Pa Ma Ga Re Sa.

Pakaṛ : Re Ma Pa Dha, Dha Pa Ma Ga Re, Ni Ga Re Ga Re Sa.

Chalan : (1) Sa Re Ma, Pa Dha Pa Ma Ga Re, Ga Re Sa

(2) Sa Re Ma Pa Dha, Ni Dha Pa Ma Ga Re Ga Re, Ni Ga, Re Ga Re Sa

(3) Ma Pa Dha Ni Sa Sa Ni Dha Pa Dha Ni, Ni Sa Ni, Dha Pa Ma Pa Dha, Pa Dha Pa Ma Ga Re, Ga Re, Ga Re Sa.

(4) Ma Pa Dha Ni Sa Re Sa, Ni Ga Re Sa, Re Sa Ni Dha, Dha Pa Ni, Ni, Pa Ma Pa Dha, Dha Dha Pa Ma Ga Re, Ma Pa Ma Ga Re Ga Re Sa Ni Ga Re Sa.

(5) Ni Sa Re Sa, Ni Ga Ga Sa, Sa Re Ma, Ma Pa Ma Ga Re Ga Re, Sa Dha Pa Ni, Dha Pa Ma Ga Re Ga Re, Ni Sa Re Sa.

(6) Dha, Dha Ni Dha, Sa Ni Dha, Dha Pa Ni, Dha Pa Ma Ga Re Ga Re, Re Dha Dha Pa Ma Ga Re, Ga Re, Ni Ga Re Sa.

9

Conclusion

In the present scenario we are all obsessed with the modern technology without which we cannot survive and hardly have the time to learn a *rāga* for more than a year or so from a *guru*. Radio and Television are the most popular media for the propagation of our music and also partly make the artistes widely known too. As a result the *gharānā* system is fast losing its ground which was not visualized by our great masters. Today, a serious student of music can listen to any artistes through these electronic media and any other resources such as tape-recorder, CD, cassettes, etc. The relevance of *gharānā* system today having been pushed to the backwaters, we all need to ponder over the issue for its possible revival. We hardly can distinguish the modern generation of players as to who is the follower of which *gharānā*. It is difficult to distinguish a *gharānā* in general but there are still some artistes who are holding the fort with pride and prejudice. But music is a performing art and it has to flow ceaselessly like a fountain and it cannot stop at any point of time. Thus it has to flourish and bloom, and who knows we may have a new *gharānā* system evolving out of these and we may reach new horizons in the domain of Indian classical music.

With the advent of modern technology, we are certainly losing our old tradition of being respectful to our elders and *guru*s. In the modern times, there is a tendency of avoiding the names of the *guru*s who shaped their *śiṣya*s'(students') musical attainments.

The reason can be well determined; in the olden days the *śiṣya*s had to go through a thousand *parīkṣā*s (tests) before the *guru* accepted them as his disciples. But today, if a *guru* tells a student that I will teach you a *rāga* in one year, then the instant reaction will be that the *śiṣya* will go to another *guru*, or he will accept any gadget like the radio or tape-recorder or even a CD player as his *guru*. That is why that the importance of *gharānā* system and *guru-śiṣya` paramparā* must be carried forward for the sake of our great tradition. My *gurujī* used to tell me stories of the past and one of them is that if any artiste was singing a *rāga* without having learnt it properly from an established *guru*, the connoisseurs would immediately know and ask the performer in public — *kyā ye rāga Sīkhī-hui-hai . . . yā sunī-hui-hai* (Have you learnt this *rāga* from a *guru* or have you just listened it). Today the most dangerous trend in classical music is that no well learned or famous musician goes to listen to other performers. As a result, there is no one to ask the performing artiste any question nor does the artiste bother "in the absence of any learned musician"to present a performance with proper attention and care. The word *tālīm* has already faded away from the domain of Indian classical music as also the importance of the *gharānā* system of yester years.

Today we find a sea change in the attitude and approach towards our age old traditions by our performers and it is their strong belief that we must not stick to one particular style or tradition. Music has now come out in the open from the *darbār*s of *mahārājā*s and *nawāb*s, we just therefore, embrace whatever is good in others. As a result of this free for all approach it becomes difficult to identify one's lineage and *gharānā* from ones performance. The present younger generation is looking forward to a better music and perfection with a little bit of modern touch, because it is no more for the chosen few but for the masses. I have heard some young turks of today who say, why should they not do what the masses want of them and why to follow the tradition if the audiences want something else? Is the *antarā* of a *bandiś* so essential or necessary to enjoy the music, or, is the application of a particular note with proper *śruti*, as laid down in our Śāstras and taught by the great masters unavoidable to uphold the principles and aesthetics of a *rāga*?

Why should we not use the embellishment, as *khaṭkā*, *krintan*, *murkī* even if it is not allowed in a *rāga*, in order to maintain the spirit and sentiments of it? Because of the evolution of music and change in technique, the presentation of a recital is passing through a changing phase. The time alone will tell whether we have done the right thing or not. But our tradition will go on and it can never be buried, in the name of modernism. *Rāga*s like Toḍī, Yaman, Darbārī, Jaunpurī, Purya, Bhairvī, Jaījaīvantī and many others, have survived the worst of times, and tradition has proved it beyond doubt that certain things in our tradition and music cannot be washed away in the name of mere creativity or modernism. But creativity and tradition has to and shall survive in our music. Because our music is based on the foundations of Vedic *paramparā* we are proud that India has given this precious knowledge "*Veda*" to the world. It is our duty to preserve our culture and music which are based on Vedas, so that the future generations may be benefited from having some exposure to our great and rich cultural traditions including music.

The art of classical music, from which we have inherited this culture, is based on "oral tradition" (*maukhik paramparā*). Our music still lives because of this tradition, which we call *guru-śiṣya paramparā*; if we have succeeded in maintaining this richest traditional art form, it is only because of our *gurus*. This is that kind of music which cannot be explained in writing alone because our notation system is not that perfect and developed so as to explicitly describe the application of the finest frequencies of a note in a particular *rāga*.

As I have said earlier, the importance and value of the peculiar tradition of *gharānā* system is fast fading away because of modern influences and invention of technical equipments. It will be perhaps a good idea, if we or our great masters could collectively find time to work out a clear interpretation of a *bandiś* (composition) with a mechanical reproduction. Pandit Bhatkhande's *Kramik Pustak Mālikā* has been a great help for the students of music, but unfortunately, as of now there are no practical demonstrations of those invaluable compositions of Bhatkhande. Without the performing aspect of these compositions, or for that matter any composition by any of the great masters, our effort to revive the tradition will be incomplete.

I hope and pray that a day will come when our notation system and the compfositions written by the great masters can be supplemented with recordings as a supportive measure to reach out to our future generations with a bouqet of our rich heritage. Thus, our traditional music and compositions will not only be widely understood by the students of music but it also shall survive and flourish forever.